Stanley's Back!

The Detroit Red Wings recapture the Cup in 2002

The Detroit News

The Detroit News

EDITORS

MARK SILVERMAN, *Publisher and Editor*
EVERETT J. MITCHELL II, *Managing Editor*
SUSAN BURZYNSKI, *Associate Editor*
NOLAN FINLEY, *Editorial Page Editor*

BOOK CREDITS

RICHARD EPPS, *Editor*
RICHARD EPPS AND ERIC MILLIKIN, *Cover and book design*
STEVE FECHT, *Director of Photography*
ED BALLOTTS, *Photo Editor*
JAN LOVELL, *Imaging*
JIM RUSS AND BRIAN HOFFMAN, *Copy Editors*

SPORTS PUBLISHING, L.L.C.

PETER L. BANNON, *Publisher*
JOSEPH J. BANNON, JR. AND SUSAN M. MOYER, *Senior Managing Editors*
K. JEFFERY HIGGERSON, *Art Director*

Hard cover ISBN: 1-58261-597-7

Soft cover ISBN: 1-58261-555-1

Published by Sports Publishing L.L.C.

Typefaces: FB Californian, Giza, Poynter Gothic
Printed in the United States

Contents

PHOTO: DANIEL MEARS

Chris Chelios shows his appreciation to Red Wings owners Mike and Marian Ilitch.

COVER PHOTO BY DANIEL MEARS
PAGE 2 PHOTO BY DANIEL MEARS
BACK COVER PHOTO BY DAVID GURALNICK

Darren McCarty and his son Griffin, 6, celebrate the team's Stanley Cup victory.

This year's Wings add to special hockey tradition

BY MR. HOCKEY, GORDIE HOWE

What is tradition? It's respect and memories. It is the numbers hanging over the ice at Joe Louis Arena as the Red Wings won the Stanley Cup. The No. 12 for Sid Abel, No. 1 for Terry Sawchuk, No. 7 for Ted Lindsay, No. 10 for Alex Delvecchio and my No. 9, along with all the banners for the Stanley Cup championships.

You never think you deserve it. It's part of the respect and memories. When a parent takes a kid into Joe Louis Arena and they see a banner and the kid asks, "Who's that?"

It means a lot to me. It's like winning a private trophy. The Red Wings' tradition started with Jack Adams, who was my coach and general manager when I joined the Red Wings in 1946.

It's why Jack Adams was so great. The pride is always there. The team had won three Cups when I got there, and now it has won 10. The name Howe has been on all 10 of them.

Syd Howe was the first Howe with his name on the Cup, when the Red Wings won their three championships in 1936, 1937 and 1943. He was not a relation of ours, and retired the season before I became a Red Wing.

The next four, I was on it in the 1950s. And then they put Colleen's and my son Mark's name on it when the Red Wings won the Cup in 1997 and 1998 and now again in 2002.

I liked them putting Mark's name on it as much if not more than having my name on it. Mark had some great years playing in Philadelphia, but when he had a chance to come back, he did because he wanted to wear a Red Wings uniform.

They didn't win the Cup when he was playing for the Red Wings, but they put his name on as a pro scout, his current job. There were a lot of great hockey players who never got their name on the Cup.

We always had a good relationship with the fans. Jack Adams used to come into the dressing room and say, "On Friday, Tuesday and Thursday, there are banquets. We want volunteers — Howe, Lindsay, Kelly and Pavelich."

We'd go, Ted Lindsay, Red Kelly, Marty Pavelich — we all lived in the same rooming house. I don't think I bought a meal for a month and a half.

When you meet the people, they become fans. Jack Adams was very demanding and sometimes got involved with our personal lives.

When Colleen's and my oldest son, Marty, was born in 1954, I came home from Montreal. They made the announcement of the birth after the second period in Montreal. We lost.

We had another game back home at Olympia and Jack wanted the doctor to keep Colleen and Marty at the hospital until the game was over. But they came home, and we won.

That's how Jack was — all hockey. So was Tommy Ivan. We won three Cups with him after Jack gave up coaching. We won the second of our four Cups in 1952 in eight straight.

We played only two playoff series back then, and we didn't lose a game. Terry Sawchuk had four shutouts. It was 50 years ago, and the tradition is carried on to the 2002 team that won the Cup.

Steve Yzerman? Stevie, I heard him talk after they won the Cup and he sounded like a true leader and veteran. I'm happy for him, and I'm glad they mentioned the injury to his knee, because he played with pain.

Red Kelly played with a broken foot, and the fans didn't realize that he was playing with such pain. The fans got on him. Red Kelly, we never won anything without him.

I'm glad they started doing that, revealing injuries. That was an improvement in 2002. When they were hiding injuries, there might have been six or seven players involved, but there were 20,000 people in the stands.

Tradition — Detroit always has had great goaltenders. But Terry Sawchuk and Dominik Hasek were different. Terry never had that personality. I never saw Terry jump up and down when we scored a goal. Hasek is like a kid.

And the Red Wings tradition carried on with Scotty Bowman as the coach. He's leaving. I don't like to hear that. Jack Adams, he didn't like you, he was on your butt. Scotty, he justs sits you out and let's you figure it out. Scotty's a quiet Jack Adams.

Stanley's Back!

Hockeytown Fans

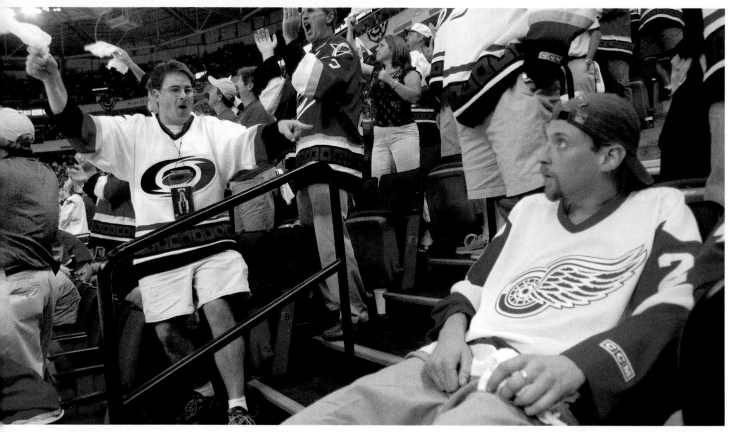

Hurricane fans taunt Keith Malcomson of Ferndale during Game 3 in Raleigh.

Sally Klebba of Hartland has her hair made up like an octopus.

Ed Gamble of Shelby Township arrives at The Joe in an outrageous octopus costume.

PHOTO: JOHN T. GREILICK

"The Fine Line" support their favorite Wings superstars. They are (from left) Becky Huetteman, 19, of Pinckney; Teresa Blankenbaker, 19, of Ypsilanti; Kristen Wiseman, 18, of Ypsilanti and Amy Wiseman, 20, of Ypsilanti.

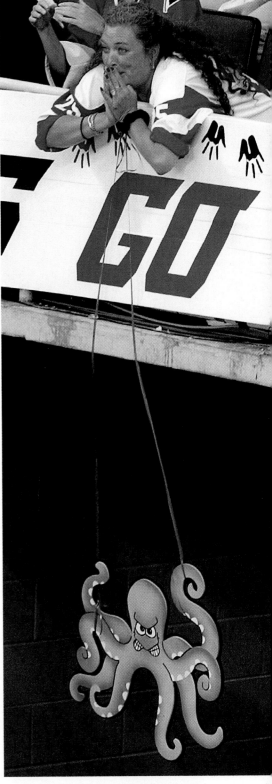

PHOTO: DANIEL MEARS

PHOTO: DANIEL MEARS

Eric Ziegler of Clinton Twp., Don Baranowski of Chesterfield Twp. and Chap Kovala of Chesterfield Twp. celebrate during Game 4 against the Blues in St. Louis.

Mary McGarrigle of Redford roots for her team in Game 4 of the Finals in Raleigh.

Yzerman's finest hour

2002 playoffs showed he's one of greatest ever

BY JERRY GREEN

T here were the barren years. How Steve Yzerman endured those times of hope and disappointment and rejection.

He has played 19 seasons in Detroit now, nearly two decades, a generation. It is in Detroit where he arrived as an ambitious teenager with a drive for hockey. It is in Detroit where he developed and matured into a leader and a man. It is in Detroit where he became one of the NHL's foremost players, in a class with Wayne Gretzky and Mario Lemieux, his contemporaries. And it is in Detroit where he watched others win the Stanley Cup, year after year, until at last the Red Wings won the championship after 42 seasons of futility.

"When I started playing as a kid, I dreamed of the NHL and the Stanley Cup," Yzerman once said. "But it was filled with a lot of disappointments, a lot of tough losses. I think I'm a better player for it."

Still, after his first two Stanley Cup championships, Yzerman could not gain the respect and the stature of a

Steve Yzerman didn't let an injury keep him from leading the Wings to another Stanley Cup.

PHOTO: DAVID GURALNICK

Stanley's Back!
Steve Yzerman

PHOTO: JOHN T. GREILICK

Steve Yzerman endured many lean years before the Wings became champions.

Gretzky or a Lemieux.

Until now. Until the spring of 2002, when he bravely led the Red Wings despite a wounded knee at age 37, cajoling teammates when they needed it, to their third Stanley Cup championship in six seasons. And the wise men of hockey gushed in praise of Yzerman, the Red Wings' captain since he was 21.

"He does not quit," said the acerbic Don Cherry to his TV hockey audience across Canada as the Red Wings were stuffing the Carolina Hurricanes in the Stanley Cup Finals. "What a guy! The best player on one leg. The captain. What a guy!"

"I personally believe Yzerman's the one who makes the difference night after night," said Barry Melrose to his TV hockey audience across the United States after the same game.

"C for Captain, C for courageous," said Harry Neale on the Canadian telecast.

"I was the one who named him captain of the Red Wings," Jacques Demers wrote in USA Today during the

"I NEVER HAD A PLAYER LIKE STEVE YZERMAN. STEVE IS PLAYING ON ONE LEG. I'M AMAZED HE CAN DO THAT. I'M REALLY AMAZED."

Scotty Bowman, on his 2002 playoff performance

playoffs, "and I never looked back. They thought maybe he was too young. But some athletes take the profession very seriously. Each game is a challenge for them. That's Steve Yzerman. This man doesn't play for money. He plays for pride. He plays for his team. He looks to win championships."

No faint praise here. Each of these admirers of Steve Yzerman had been an NHL coach — and each had consid-

Under Scotty Bowman, Steve Yzerman was transformed into a complete, two-way player.

erable success in playoff hockey.

And then there were the comments during the playoffs from Scotty Bowman: "I never had a player like Steve Yzerman. Steve is playing on one leg. I'm amazed he can do that. I'm really amazed."

Once, during those barren years, Mike Keenan, another prominent coach, disqualified Yzerman when selecting a Team Canada side for international competition. Now Yzerman has won an Olympic gold medal and the Stanley Cup in the same year. He played in the Olympics with the same determination as he played in the 2002 playoffs. With the same gimpy right knee.

PHOTO: DAVID GURALNICK

The Wings, led by captain Steve Yzerman, forced the Blues to make a quick exit in the second round.

He underwent arthroscopic surgery on the knee in January. And in February he was on the ice, for Canada, at Salt Lake City. He took his regular shift for the Canadian team — and on that special Sunday, after victory over the USA, he smiled as a gold medal was wrapped around his neck. But the knee was painful. And in March, he was unable to skate.

The Detroit critics — talk radio motor mouths and fans — roasted him for endangering himself, and the Wings, by insisting on playing in the Olympics. But when the playoffs started in April, Captain Yzerman was there, again, leading.

"Let's face it," teammate Kris Draper said, "the man loves this time of year. He elevates his game and elevates everyone around him. He's grabbed this team and led the way, like he always does."

And the Red Wings were a team that needed to be grabbed.

They were a team constructed to win the Stanley Cup. After bitter disappointment in the spring of 2001, owner Mike Ilitch dug deeply to bolster his hockey team. The Wings had been upset in the first round by the Los Angeles Kings — largely because Yzerman and Brendan Shanahan were injured. Over the summer, general manager Ken Holland added Dominik Hasek to play goal, and Luc Robitaille and Brett Hull to score goals. To soften Ilitch's financial burden, Yzerman was one of the players restructuring his contract.

The team — always the team.

Then, after dominating the NHL throughout the 2001-02 season, the Red Wings opened the playoffs with two

PHOTO: DAVID GURALNICK

Former coach Jacques Demers named Steve Yzerman captain when Yzerman was 21.

flops. They lost twice to the Vancouver Canucks. They had been beaten and embarrassed, their quest for the Cup in jeopardy.

It was then, in Vancouver, before Game 3 of the first round, that Captain Yzerman stood and challenged his teammates — as he had during playoff troubles in other years. Basically, he told the Wings they were too good to lose to Vancouver.

Indeed, these aged, experienced, star-laden Red Wings dropped behind lesser clubs in three of their four playoff series en route to the Stanley Cup. Each time they rallied. They won four successive games, after Yzerman's speech, to oust Vancouver. They whipped the St. Louis Blues, as usual. Then they struggled vs. the archrival Colorado Avalanche, down 3-2 before winning the final two games to reach the Finals. And in the Finals there was the early drop into the doldrums, losing the first game to the Carolina Hurricanes before winning the Cup.

"We're not discouraged by losing a game," Yzerman said when asked about the Wings' knack of overcoming adver-

PHOTO: JOHN T. GREILICK

Steve Yzerman scored 50 or more goals five times in his NHL career.

Stanley's Back!

Steve Yzerman

Injuries to Steve Yzerman and Brendan Shanahan cut short the Wings' playoff run in 2001, but they bounced back in a big way in 2002.

sity. "We're determined to stick with what we're trying to accomplish. We stick with what we're doing."

No panic.

"He doesn't get headlines, but it's terrifying to see him on the ice in the playoffs," Vancouver general manager Brian Burke said.

He is terrifying, yet so different now from the barren years. Yzerman was a prolific scorer at the beginning, but his goals never won any championships. Five times he reached the illustrious 50-goal mark, scoring 65 in the 1988-89 season.

One day while all this was going on, he confessed his emotions in a dark room in the catacombs inside Joe Louis Arena.

"As long as I remember, since I was 5 years old, I watched the playoffs," he said that day, in the early 1990s. "No matter what I'm doing, no matter what I've seen or missed of the

playoffs, I always made a point of seeing the final game — or the end of the final game — because I enjoy seeing the Stanley Cup presented.

"I've got friends who've won the Cup and it's interesting to see people when they win and how they react. To see them in the summer and ask what it was like. ... Very envious. ... I always dreamed that maybe I'd get there."

Then, in 1997, he did. The barren years had ended. To do it, to become a champion, he was forced to change. Bowman was hired to coach the Red Wings in 1993. He soon tinkered with Yzerman's style.

"His second season, Scotty called us together and said, 'We're going to be a defensive team, and everybody's going to be accountable,'" Yzerman said. "I made a conscious effort to change. To play well or effectively, I had to change.

"The motivation was to win. It didn't matter how many goals I scored, how many points I scored. We got stronger

Wings captain Steve Yzerman leaves the Joe with the Stanley Cup in hand.

and stronger. The hardest part was to go five games without a point or a goal and say, 'I played a good game.' You've got to swallow your pride.

"Scotty said, 'Nothing else matters but winning. Who scored doesn't matter.'"

Bowman's philosophy molded the Red Wings into a championship team — three times over now. Yzerman took the Cup in the presentation at center ice his first time in 1997. He skated around the ice with it. The dream he had since he was 5 had come true.

In the dressing room, in the celebration, he talked quietly in a corner, jammed by journalists. There was a mob.

Yzerman stood out front among the crowd as cham-

pagne spurted through the room. He wore a cap that read: "Stanley Cup CHAMPS."

And he spoke again from the heart.

"I love this team," he said, a champion at last.

A year later, in 1998, Yzerman lugged the Stanley Cup around a second time. But even with two championships, he never quite received the recognition he deserved from around the league.

Now that is over, too. Playing on one leg, with a wounded knee, Yzerman has been awarded the respect he deserves around the league. He is a certified star.

The 2002 playoffs showed Steve Yzerman at his very finest.

The Road to the Playoffs
Hall of Fame team

The 2001-02 Red Wings are introduced
to the Joe Louis Arena crowd for the
first time at this season's opener
against Calgary.

PHOTO: DAVID GURALNICK

Bold stroke brings Hasek

Red Wings get six-time Vezina Trophy winner

By Bob Wojnowski

Just like that, the Red Wings are dangerous again. Just like that, with a midnight stroke that brought them goaltender Dominik Hasek, the Wings are intriguing again.

The focus of an experienced team changed but the point didn't, and it shouldn't. The point is, the Wings still think they can contend now, and they'll grow old trying, if they must.

You don't turn down a chance to get the best, no matter the risk. It's the philosophy that first brought Scotty Bowman here eight years ago, and it's the one that landed Hasek.

As long as you have a high-priced team with veteran stars, led by 36-year-old captain Steve Yzerman and 67-year-old legend Bowman, it makes no sense to back off and rebuild. Be honest. No matter what you think of Hasek, an enigmatic 36-year-old six-time Vezina Trophy winner, or how many other areas the Wings still need to upgrade, you're fascinated to see how he fits. You're not the only one.

"Going into the playoffs next year, everybody's going to say they don't want to play the Red Wings in the first round, and the sole reason will be because of Hasek," Yzerman said. "We've got a goalie who can win any game any time, and win a playoff series by himself. Has it made us younger? No. Has it made us better? I'd have to say so."

That's no intentional rip on Chris Osgood, who never got enough credit for the Wings' second Stanley Cup, and now will be traded. You feel bad for Osgood, who seldom was as shaky as his critics suggested, although he did struggle last season. Then, when the team collapsed around him, Osgood couldn't steal that first-round series from Los Angeles.

You might even shed a tear for the loss of that great Detroit rarity, a first-round draft pick. But I'm sorry, if you have a chance to get one of the finest goalies of a generation, you do it.

The Red Wings weren't the only NHL team that made a move in preparation for a run at the Stanley Cup. Defending champion Colorado re-signed forward Joe Sakic, goaltender Patrick Roy and defenseman Rob Blake to multiyear deals.

What's more, St. Louis acquired All-Star center Doug Weight, a Warren native, from Edmonton, and the Dallas Stars signed free-agent center Pierre Turgeon, who had been with the Blues.

That's why General Manager Ken Holland boldly snatched Hasek, who might play only one more year, although he's not far from his prime. Actually, I bet he'll get here, see all the players packed into the same age and tax brackets, and want to stay longer.

"He's an impact guy, an impact on a team, an impact on the league," Yzerman said. "It's a real coup for our organization."

So the Wings aren't getting younger or cheaper, which is fine, as long as they're getting better. And yes, acquiring Hasek for Vyacheslav Kozlov, a 2002 first-round pick and future considerations, makes them better now, if not in 2005. As they watched their Western Conference rivals load up to win now, the Wings had no choice.

This is a move Holland had to make once it became apparent Hasek wanted out of Buffalo. It didn't cost the Wings exorbitantly in trade or in contract ($8 million per season). It also shouldn't preclude Holland from making other deals because the Wings still have large holes, especially on defense. The price for Philadelphia's Eric Lindros will continue to drop as the summer unfolds. Less expensive free-agent defensemen could suffice because supreme talents aren't mandatory when you have "The Dominator."

We certainly can ditch the notion that Holland was too interested in standing pat. In a league in which fewer top teams divvy up more and more of the talent, cleverness and

20

Dominik Hasek's arrival meant the end of Chris Osgood's time in Detroit.

guts are required. Holland showed both. The free-agent market is way too volatile to count on. Colorado immediately re-signed Joe Sakic, Patrick Roy and Rob Blake. Philadelphia already grabbed Jeremy Roenick and might swipe Martin Lapointe from the Wings, which would be a blow. Dallas signed Pierre Turgeon. St. Louis traded for Doug Weight.

"We felt good about our goaltending," Holland said, "but when a goalie of Dominik Hasek's stature becomes available to you, you have to react."

Reaction comes with cost, obviously. Hasek led the league with 11 shutouts but struggled early in the season. Also, because everything happened in a whirlwind, Holland left himself with little leverage to deal Osgood. Teams know the Wings can't keep Hasek, Osgood and Manny Legace, so Holland could have trouble getting fair value for Osgood.

Osgood's biggest crime, strangely, was his consistency. When the Wings needed spectacular, usually he was just good. The older they get, the more competitive the elite teams become, the more often the Wings now need spectacular.

Hasek is the hope and the risk. He's a legitimate hope. He's worth the risk.

Free-agent acquisition Brett Hull brought a much-needed scoring threat to the Red Wings.

Hull fits in Hockeytown

Holland: Chemistry won't be a problem for team

> **WE'RE TALKING ABOUT A FUTURE HALL OF FAMER, A HOUSEHOLD NAME IN THE SPORT OF HOCKEY AND SOMEONE WHO CAN ELECTRIFY AN ARENA."**
> **Mike Barnett, Brett Hull's agent**

BY TED KULFAN

The addition of Brett Hull gives the Red Wings another dynamic, high-powered personality in a locker room brimming with them.

With NHL dignitaries such as Steve Yzerman, Brendan Shanahan, Dominik Hasek, Luc Robitaille, Chris Chelios and Sergei Fedorov, (along with soft-spoken Norris Trophy winner Nicklas Lidstrom), the Wings will be a traveling collection of future Hall of Famers this season.

General Manager Ken Holland said with so many big names, and many new players, team chemistry could be a concern. "You're always worried about chemistry," Holland said. "I would say that's one thing that will need to come together as we look ahead. It will be a challenge. Things such as ice time, who'll see the time on the power play. But as I sit here now, I feel we have a group of players (for whom) things like that will not be an issue."

Hull, 37, who signed a two-year, $9-million contract Wednesday, brings a different dynamic to the Wings.

Hull, among the most outspoken, high-profile players in the league, has never shied away from expressing his feelings about how league issues affect players.

Hull also reportedly had a rift with Stars Coach Ken Hitchcock that led, in part, to the Stars not re-signing him as an unrestricted free agent this summer.

Holland said he isn't concerned about Hull's personality fitting into the Wings' fabric.

"We've got a strong group of veteran leaders in that locker room led by Steve Yzerman," Holland said. "We have a strong-willed, veteran coach who has been extremely successful. I don't think any of that will be an issue.

"I've talked with Brett, and he has nothing but respect for the people such as Chris Chelios, Yzerman, and players like that. It meant a lot when he chose to play for the Wings, rather than other places where he could have earned more money. He wanted to be part of this team, this group of players."

Former Stars teammate Mike Modano said Hull should adjust nicely in Detroit. "It's great for him. Of the teams he was talking to, I think he'll have the most fun there," Modano told the Dallas Morning News. "They've got some great playmakers, and he's going to get a chance to play with some fantastic players."

Hull cherished the idea of returning to Dallas, where he scored 39 goals last year, enjoyed the weather, and had a good rapport with his teammates. But the Stars were adamant about offering a one-year deal for much less than the $7-million option they refused to pick up after last season.

Hull and his agent, Mike Barnett, were looking for a two-year contract. "(Hull) knows the commitment it takes in May and June to get to the Finals to win a Cup," Barnett said. "He scores an enormous amount of even-strength goals, a true indicator of a great goal-scorer. We're talking about a future Hall of Famer, a household name in the sport of hockey and someone who can electrify an arena with an evening of goal-scoring."

There was concern in Dallas whether Hitchcock and Hull could coexist for another season. The two clashed about Hitchcock's conservative offensive system during the course of Hull's three seasons in Dallas.

But Hitchcock recently told the Dallas Morning News he appreciated what Hull did with the Stars.

"As much as I think Brett Hull learned from us, we learned a lot from Brett Hull," Hitchcock said.

PHOTO: DAVID GURALNICK

Luc Robitaille signed a two-year, $9-million free-agent contract with Detroit in hopes of completing his Hall of Fame resume with a Stanley Cup championship.

24

Luc leaves L.A.

Robitaille's quest for Cup continues with Wings after Kings make unattractive offer

By John Niyo

uc Robitaille has always been a bit slow.

He was traded to the Pittsburgh Penguins two years after they won their second consecutive Stanley Cup in 1992. He was traded to the New York Rangers a year after they won the Stanley Cup in 1994.

Now here he is in Detroit, where the Wings are three years removed from their recent championships.

So, yes, one would have to agree that he's a step behind.

It's also the reason Robitaille was drafted 171st overall in the 1984 draft, well behind, among others, Atlanta Braves pitcher Tom Glavine.

It's the reason he was sent packing from Pittsburgh and New York, traded despite his All-Star credentials.

And it's the reason he's here in Hockeytown after signing a two-year, $9-million free agent contract last week.

The Kings, looking to trim payroll and create a lineup centered around youth and speed, made only one contract offer this summer to Robitaille, a fan favorite in Los Angeles ever since his Calder Trophy-winning season as a rookie in 1986.

The Kings' offer: A one-year deal at a reduced salary of $2.5 million next season.

As bids go, it was a farewell. Robitaille's co-agent, Tom Reich, told the Los Angeles Times the offer was "about as attractive as a Zamboni through your front door."

So Robitaille landed on the Wings' doorstep, where he'll join fellow newcomer Dominik Hasek in a similar quest.

Three days after Hasek told Wings fans he's here to win the Stanley Cup — "Nothing else, nothing less," he said — Robitaille used the same rallying cry.

"I came here because I want to win the Cup, no question," said Robitaille, a future Hall of Famer who ranks 13th among the NHL's all-time leaders in goals with 590.

Robitaille knows the clock is ticking. He also knows this latest contract will be his last.

But even a 15-year NHL veteran is allowed to dream. Robitaille admitted as much last week, saying he'd been glued to the television set last month, watching the tearful celebration following Game 7 of the Colorado-New Jersey finals as another future Hall of Famer hoisted the Stanley Cup.

"I watched Ray Bourque win it," said Robitaille, whose Kings were eliminated by Bourque and the Avalanche after a first-round upset of the Wings. "I watched the game all by myself and I selfishly thought, 'I wish that was me.' I was very happy for him. I want to feel the same way — lift the Cup over my head before I retire."

He proved last season he's not ready to retire just yet. Robitaille, who credits a strenuous off-season conditioning program for his continued success, led the Kings with 37 goals while playing in all 82 games in the regular season.

> ## "I CAME HERE BECAUSE I WANT TO WIN THE CUP, NO QUESTION."
> **Luc Robitaille**

He added four goals and three assists in 13 playoff games, but his defensive breakdowns continually frustrated Coach Andy Murray.

Now he's Scotty Bowman's dilemma, though it's clear Robitaille will be asked to do one thing in Detroit: score goals.

The Wings gave up 47 goals from last season when they traded Vyacheslav Kozlov to Buffalo and let Martin Lapointe leave for Boston via free agency. Robitaille, whose wife, singer/model Stacia, and sons Steven and Jesse, will remain in Los Angeles this season, should help fill that void.

He was second in the league in power-play points last season with 45. He scored 16 power-play goals, more than anyone on the Wings' roster. (Brendan Shanahan had 15.) And over the last three seasons his goal totals — 39, 36, 37 — are proof that "Lucky Luc" still has what it takes in the final years of his career.

Too little, too late? That remains to be seen.

Luc proves 'em wrong

Robitaille shows scouts were wrong about his potential

BY TED KULFAN

What does it say about NHL scouts — and the NHL draft — that Atlanta Braves pitcher Tom Glavine was selected in the seventh round in 1984, two rounds before Luc Robitaille?

What were so many scouts thinking? Or not thinking?

"And Glavine said he wasn't even going to play hockey," said Robitaille, his trademark smile going full tilt now. "Yeah, well, what can you do?"

Robitaille has had the last laugh. He's been laughing for 16 seasons now, all the way to the magical milestone of 600 career goals.

He became the third current Red Wing to reach 600, joining Brett Hull and Steve Yzerman. Only 12 players in NHL history have surpassed 600 goals.

"Obviously it's quite an honor," Robitaille said.

The Wings drafted eight players in 1984 before Robitaille was off the board: Shawn Burr, Doug Houda, Milan Chalupa, Mats Lundstrom, Randy Hansch, Stefan Larsson, Lars Karlsson and Urban Nordin.

Despite being picked so low (171st overall) in the draft, Robitaille is long past playing to prove people wrong.

"I don't think about those things anymore," Robitaille said. "That's long in the past. I'm proud of what I've accomplished."

It certainly has been an impressive career, accomplished by a player many scouts felt was too slow, too small and too

"SCOUTS HAVE A TENDENCY TO JUST CONCENTRATE ON THE PHYSICAL THINGS. THERE'S MORE TO IT THAN THAT."
Luc Robitaille

weak defensively to stick around long in the NHL.

Robitaille, who is currently listed as 6-foot-1 and 215 pounds, instead enjoys needling his friends in the scouting business these days.

"Sometimes you have to go beyond just the size, speed and shot, and those types of things," Robitaille said. "Scouts have a tendency to just concentrate on the physical things. There's more to it than that."

What Robitaille has is an uncanny ability to know where the puck is, to find the open lane in the offensive zone. He has a knack for being around the net at the right time and scoring goals in tough situations.

"When you have a puck around the net, he's going to do better than most guys," Coach Scotty Bowman said.

General Manager Ken Holland said it was an easy decision to sign Robitaille in the off-season as an unrestricted free agent, in essence replacing Vyacheslav Kozlov (traded for goalie Dominik Hasek) on left wing.

"What's made Luc the prolific scorer he is are his head, his offensive instincts, great hands, his scoring touch," Holland said. "Some people get a lot of scoring opportunities, but they need eight or 10 chances to score a goal. If Luc gets one or two, there's a pretty good chance he's going to score."

Holland loves to talk about the ability of veteran players

PHOTO: DAVID GURALNICK

Luc Robitaille and his family receive a silver stick from owners Mike and Marian Ilitch.

to find open spots on the ice. Robitaille is a good example of a player who knows how to negotiate his way into an open space and score.

"He knows where to go to be open," Holland said. "If there's a seam, if there's going to be space, he'll find it. He's made a potential Hall of Fame career from the top of the circle on down, and that's a gift. Some people know where to go and where to set up, and he's one of them."

Robitaille said Alex Schmart of the Kings was the only one who scouted him (and Red Wings defenseman Steve Duchesne, who went undrafted but signed a free-agent contract with the Kings in 1984).

"There's a good chance I would never have gotten drafted if Alex didn't scout me and the Kings didn't pick me," said Robitaille, noting that at the time, the NHL selected primarily 18-year-olds (which Robitaille was) and passed over junior over-agers (19- and 20-year-olds).

Tough to imagine a potential Hall of Fame career gone unnoticed. Or passed over by a baseball pitcher.

Stanley's Back!
Brendan Shanahan's 500th goal

Brendan Shanahan waves to the crowd after being given a silver stick, honoring the 500th goal of his career, during the Wings' 5-3 loss to the St. Louis Blues in the last game of the regular season.

Shanahan hits milestone

500th career goal lifts Wings past Avalanche

BY TED KULFAN

The Red Wings' rivalry with the Colorado Avalanche isn't dead after all.

Brendan Shanahan scored his 500th career goal in the Wings' 2-0 victory, but a mini-brawl late in the third period highlighted Saturday's afternoon game.

Shanahan broke a scoreless tie at 7:48 of the third with his 34th goal of the season on a five-on-three power play. In the left circle, Shanahan one-timed a pass from Nicklas Lidstrom and beat Avalanche goalie Patrick Roy.

"I don't know how many of those I've gotten from Nick in my career here," Shanahan said. "I'm just glad it came against a great goalie, in a big game, and it helped us win a game. That makes it more meaningful."

Shanahan showed little emotion after breaking an eight-game scoring drought.

"Like I've said before, it's just another goal," he said. "It'll mean more when I reflect on it later, but team goals have always been more exciting to me."

Shortly after Shanahan's goal, a mini-melee prompted many onlookers to think back to the Wings-Avalanche games of the late 1990s.

The trouble began at 9:56 of the third period when Kirk Maltby was pushed into the Colorado net by Avalanche defenseman Martin Skoula.

Roy took exception and began punching Maltby inside the net.

"I was going to the net and Skoula took me in," Maltby said. "I was just trying not to hit my head. Then it became a wrestling match."

Roy accused Maltby of attempting to take out his knee.

"What I didn't like is that he tried to take my knee off," Roy said. "It was clear to me because normally a guy will hit me in front, and he (Maltby) tried to hit me on top. I didn't think it was an accident. I really think he tried to hurt me."

Players from both teams began to gather around the Avalanche net when Wings goalie Dominik Hasek roared down the ice, apparently wanting to get after Roy.

Hasek slipped and took out Roy's legs from under him. Roy got up, not exactly aware of who took him to the ice, but was inviting Hasek to tangle before referees distanced the two goalies.

"I felt it was my responsibility to go there and help my teammates," Hasek said. "I was ready to fight."

Said Roy: "It would have been interesting if the ref had not been there."

The Avalanche got a power play out of the incident, for Hasek leaving the crease, but the Wings killed it.

Brett Hull's 26th goal, at 13:03, gave the Wings a 2-0 lead.

Hasek and Roy were spectacular throughout the game. With the shutout, Hasek moved ahead of Roy, 61-60, in the lead for shutouts among current goalies.

"It was a tight game. It was the way these teams have been playing," Coach Scotty Bowman said. "Both goalies were outstanding."

The Wings won three out of four from the Avalanche during the regular season.

The Avalanche were without forwards Peter Forsberg (ankle), Milan Hejduk (abdominal), Stephane Yelle (shoulder), Dan Hinote (foot) and Steven Reinprecht (bruised foot).

"They were missing some key people," Shanahan said. "They'll be a different team as they get those people back healthy."

Golden Wings

Yzerman, Shanahan win gold for Canada

BY BOB WOJNOWSKI

Canada can breathe again. Ready, eh? Deep in, deep out. The natural order has been restored.

Steve Yzerman and Brendan Shanahan can go home again. Wayne Gretzky can smile again. And yes, Chris Chelios and Brett Hull can be proud of the Americans' effort again. And finally, after the strangest 10 days of their professional careers, the Red Wings can be teammates again.

Canada rules the hockey world after an emotional 5-2 victory over the United States in the gold-medal game Sunday, a natural conclusion to a most unnatural Winter Olympics. Canada won behind tough defense, as well as the brilliant pushing of Yzerman and the admirable guts of Shanahan. It won despite the determined pulling of Chelios and the accurate sniping of Brett Hull.

Wings pushed one way and Wings pulled the other, and after all the tugging, it ended as it should. Canada was better — bigger, stronger and a bit more desperate.

Relief? It was etched everywhere. It was on the face of Shanahan, even as his right thumb ached, busted and bandaged. Everyone knew there would be a price, and this is it.

Olympic Wings Steve Yzerman, from left, Chris Chelios, Brett Hull and Brendan Shanahan.

PHOTO: DANIEL MEARS

PHOTO: DANIEL MEARS

The Red Wings' Brett Hull, playing for the United States, tries a wrap-around against Finland.

"Painkillers mixed with adrenaline," Shanahan said, holding up the thumb that was broken against Finland. "The doctor said he didn't think there was a risk of injuring it further. It was just a matter of playing with the pain."

Playing with the pain. Canada has done it for 50 years. Mostly, it was the pain of seeing gold go elsewhere and watching its national game bleed southward, Americanized and commercialized.

Playing with the pain. Yzerman underwent arthroscopic knee surgery last month but couldn't miss this. As good as Joe Sakic was, Yzerman played as well as anyone, energized partly by national pride and partly by the rush of superb competition.

After he jumped out of the penalty box late in the third period and threaded a perfect pass to Jarome Iginla for the goal that

> **"IT'S HARD TO CONTAIN YOUR EMOTIONS. GUYS WERE TRYING TO BE ALL CALM AND STOIC, BUT YOU CAN'T. YOU LET IT LOOSE. YOU BECOME A KID AGAIN, AND THE BOYISHNESS JUST COMES OUT."**
> **Steve Yzerman**

PHOTO: DANIEL MEARS

Canadian teammates Brendan Shanahan and Mario Lemieux pose with their gold medals.

made it 4-2, Yzerman leaped, once, twice, into Iginla's arms. And you didn't have to ask what gold meant to the Captain.

"It's hard to contain your emotions," Yzerman said, the medal hanging from his neck. "Guys were trying to be all calm and stoic, but you can't. You let it loose. You become a kid again, and the boyishness just comes out."

In the end, they all pretty much got what they came to get. Yzerman and Shanahan wanted to be part of Canadian history, members of the first Olympic championship team since 1952. You can't live in Detroit without enduring a few playful Canadian pokes. But on the issue of hockey, it was time for the snickering to stop.

Speaking of snickering, it's time to let go of the Americans' 1998 debacle in Nagano, Japan. Chelios wanted redemption, and he got it. He distinguished himself as a tremendous leader and probably a future coach, the perfect captain for Herb Brooks' veteran team. Hull, with a team-high eight points, showed he was more than just a big name with a big shot.

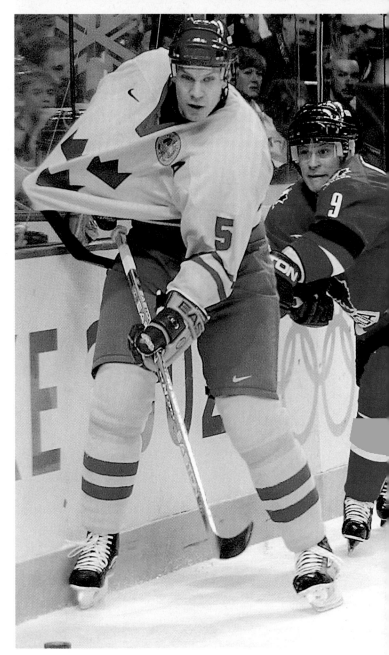

PHOTO: DANIEL MEARS

Red Wings defenseman Nicklas Lidstrom, playing for Sweden, reaches for the puck against Canada.

"I'm not sad, I'm not upset, I'm just disappointed," Chelios said. "But I've got no complaints. We got beat by the better team. I'm proud of the way we represented the United States. And I'm happy for Yzerman and Shanny. I've been growing up with those guys and been through the wars with them. I'm proud of them, too."

Chelios and Yzerman had talked frequently on cell

The Red Wings' Sergei Fedorov, center, played for Russia, which won the bronze medal.

phones, and bumped into each other in the Olympic Village. They talked of how great it would be to meet in the gold medal game. But when it happened, they wondered if they really wanted it, after all.

Make no mistake. NHL teammates didn't let up on each other. Shanahan rubbed Chelios into the boards at one point. But it was odd, they admitted, and it was too bad only two Wings got to celebrate. At Yzerman's request, all four posed for a postgame photo.

"It was wild all week, just the look we'd give each other in the cafeteria," Chelios said. "Unfortunately, with so many of us here, someone had to win, and someone had to lose."

And I imagine, someone will start talking about it in the Detroit dressing room. They might want to go easy on Nicklas Lidstrom, star of the stunned Swedish team, and Czech goaltender Dominik Hasek, also eliminated early.

But, Yzerman and Shanahan and the rest of the Canadians had the most to lose. That helps to explain the painkillers, and Yzerman's multiple leaps.

"You're secluded in the Athlete's Village so you don't realize the pressure back home," Yzerman said. "Canadians are like everybody else. They love to win. But if we had lost, it's not like they wouldn't let us back in the country. They let us come home in '98."

He laughed, or sighed, not sure which.

"Hey, the Americans played great," he added. "We won one game, and we won the right game, but it doesn't really prove dominance."

Coupled with the Canadian women's gold-medal victory over the U.S., it should keep Don Cherry chirping for another four years. Besides, Americans had become medal-gluttonous at these Olympics anyhow.

Yzerman and Shanahan did what they had to do, and got what they had to get. They're excused for dampening the U.S. fervor. And if they help win the next little tournament that begins in a couple months, they're forgiven forever.

34

PHOTO: DANIEL MEARS

Steve Yzerman congratulates Canadian goalie Martin Brodeur of the New Jersey Devils.

**Dominik Hasek makes a save
on Vancouver's Artem Chubarov
in the third period of Game 6.**

PHOTO: DAVID GURALNICK

The first step

Canucks work overtime

Sedin's soft goal past Hasek seals OT stunner

A shot by the Canucks' Henrik Sedin eludes Dominik Hasek at 13:59 of overtime. The puck appeared to deflect off the leg of Igor Larionov.

PHOTOS: DANIEL MEARS

By Ted Kulfan

The Vancouver Canucks won't be pushovers.

Henrik Sedin scored at 13:59 of overtime Wednesday night to give the Canucks a 4-3 victory over the Red Wings in Game 1 of a Western Conference quarterfinal series.

Canucks	4
Red Wings	3
Canucks lead, 1-0	

The Wings, prohibitive favorites heading into the best-of-seven series, suddenly are in trouble.

Sedin lifted a shot that deflected off Igor Larionov's pants leg and over the left shoulder of goalie Dominik Hasek.

"I've never scored in overtime," Sedin said. "I rarely ever score, so it was a pretty big goal."

The Wings led three times, including 3-2 in the third period, but couldn't hang on.

"When you get the lead in the third period, that's a game you have to sit on," Coach Scotty Bowman said.

Game 2 of the best-of-seven series is at 7 p.m. Friday at Joe Louis Arena. The series shifts to Vancouver for games 3 and 4 on Sunday and Tuesday.

"We knew these guys would come out hard," said Luc Robitaille, whose goal off a nice pass from Steve Yzerman gave the Wings a 1-0 first-period lead. "They're hungry and they've been playing well."

Sergei Fedorov (power play) and Larionov also scored for the Wings. Todd Warriner, Andrew Cassels (power play) and Trevor Linden got the other goals for the Canucks.

Linden's goal at 10:47 of the third period tied the score at 3. The Canucks capitalized after the Wings couldn't get the puck out of their zone. Linden lifted the shot in the direction of Hasek, who didn't seem to get a good look at it.

Hasek, who struggled in the final two regular-season games, was sharper but not at his best.

Warriner's goal over Hasek's left shoulder was off a shot Hasek normally stops. He made a key save on Cassels in the third period with the Wings leading, 3-2.

Dominik Hasek watches Trevor Linden celebrate after scoring in the third period.

Red-Faced

Eighth-seeded Canucks have Wings on the ropes after 5-2 victory

By Dave Dye

When the Red Wings began marketing this year's playoff slogan, "Let 'Em See Red," it wasn't supposed to mean red from embarrassment.

Canucks	5
Red Wings	2
Canucks lead, 2-0	

But that's how it looks now. The Wings, the NHL's top regular-season team, trail the Western Conference's No. 8 seed, Vancouver, two games to none in a best-of-seven series following Friday's 5-2 loss at Joe Louis Arena.

A heroic performance by Steve Yzerman and a 36-20 advantage in shots weren't enough for the Wings, who left shortly after the game for Vancouver, where Game 3 will be played Sunday.

The Canucks scored twice on deflections — that's four in two games — but Wings goalie Dominik Hasek has been shaky nonetheless. His teammates defended him.

"It's tough to blame Dom for all those goals," defenseman Nick Lidstrom said.

But Wings fans were blaming Hasek, not only booing him but also mocking him with cheers when he made an easy save.

"I don't want to use any excuse," said Hasek, who was acquired before the season with hopes that he would be the difference in a Stanley Cup run. "Ten shots, three goals (in the first two periods). It's not a good feeling. I have to work

PHOTO: DAVID GURALNICK

Vancouver defenseman Scott Lachance makes sure Steve Yzerman stays out of the play.

through it."

Todd Bertuzzi, Andrew Cassels, Scott Lachance, Markus Naslund and Matt Cooke (empty net) scored for the Canucks. Lidstrom and Yzerman got the Wings' goals.

Despite the shocking two-game deficit, the Wings didn't act afterward as if their confidence was destroyed.

"Some funny goals killed us," Yzerman said. "Weird goals. If some of the deflections go our way, we'll be right back in it. I felt we played reasonably well. If we stick with it, we feel it will turn our way."

The Wings, who had 19 turnovers to the Canucks' four, are winless in their last nine games, including an 0-5-2 finish in the regular season. They were 1-for-5 on the power play for the second straight game.

The highlight Friday was unquestionably the performance of Yzerman, who left the arena limping because of

Kirk Maltby checks Vancouver defenseman Bryan Helmer into the Red Wings' bench.

his injured right knee.

"It shows how much guts he has," Naslund said.

Said Wings Coach Scotty Bowman: "He was great. For somebody who hasn't practiced (much), he showed what kind of player he is. He showed a lot of patience and a lot of determination. We've been able to get a lot of hockey out of him."

Yzerman said he remains hindered by a brace that he's wearing to protect his ailing knee.

"I'm a little bit stiff," he said. "It's kind of cumbersome. It makes getting up difficult."

Yzerman keeps picking himself up, and now the Wings have to do the same themselves.

Kirk Maltby jostles with the Canucks' Todd Bertuzzi in the first period. Bertuzzi was a physical presence all game.

PHOTO: DAVID GURALNICK

42

Turning point

Resurgent Red Wings clamp down on Canucks

By Bob Wojnowski

Something had to start, or something surely was going to end. So the Red Wings, pushed to desperation by a feisty upstart, went back to what they knew, back to the start, and officially (finally) announced their arrival in the series.

They went back to their captain, Steve Yzerman, who again displayed wounded-knee brilliance.

They went back to their shaken goalie, Dominik Hasek, suddenly spectacular again. Hasek sealed it with a stop of Todd Bertuzzi on a penalty shot, perhaps announcing the return of the Dominator.

They went back to familiar lines and a tighter defense, a return to normalcy that lifted them past Vancouver, 3-1. Now, the series really starts, with the Canucks ahead two games to one and probably wondering if the Big Red is awake for good.

The Wings had better be awake for good. They'll need more determination, more of the misplaced elements that reappeared Sunday night. They need to be themselves, precisely the message Yzerman hammered in a meeting the day before the game.

"He said things we all knew, that this is a confident club, so there's no sense doubting ourselves," Kris Draper said. "We all realized it, but it was good to hear it from him. When he grabs this team, you go with it."

We're not sure if it officially qualifies as an inspirational instant classic, but something turned the Wings. And yes, for all their talk about bad breaks, they collected their share of fortunate ones. Nicklas Lidstrom's center-ice slapper in the final minute of the second period slipped past Dan Cloutier for the go-ahead goal, and Cloutier struggled to recover.

A return to normalcy? Maybe. Cloutier certainly returned to human status, also getting beat by Brendan Shanahan early in the third.

Yzerman had pleaded for calm, and he quickly showed why he's so confident. Leadership starts with performance, and the Wings' best started performing. If you wondered how to measure what Yzerman means to this team, just watch a tape of this game. He logged more minutes (19:55) than any Detroit forward, was poised and determined, and soothed early fears by scoring the game's first goal.

"We've played better in each game, and that's a good sign," Yzerman said. "I think we've finally caught up to playoff mode. But we've got to keep it rolling."

This was a dangerous time, and the Wings knew it. As the game started, signs of doom were everywhere. The Wings had crumbled in the past three playoffs after falling behind. The Canucks were energized. And the crowd was absolutely lit. One sign, hung from the arena balcony, said it succinctly: "Overpaid and Outplayed — Dead Wings."

Everything had been turned upside down, and it was up to the Wings to turn it back. Something would end or something would start, and in a dominant first period, they were fiercely intent on getting started.

Red Wings 3
Canucks 1
Canucks lead, 2-1

Scotty Bowman went back to old lines and familiar ways. The Grind Line — Darren McCarty, Draper, Kirk Maltby — was back together. So were the Two Kids and a Goat — Boyd Devereaux, Pavel Datsyuk, Brett Hull. So was the superstar line — Yzerman, Sergei Fedorov, Shanahan.

But if the Wings were truly to climb back, the best-tested way was the traditional way, with a twist: A one-legged captain shall lead them. OK. So Yzerman is one-kneed, not one-legged. But really, if he keeps playing at this pace, while wearing a bulky brace to support a balky right knee, we'll have to rewrite his top heroics.

Yzerman quieted the wild crowd and gave the Wings a 1-0 lead with a workmanlike play. Sound familiar? On the power play (a penalty Yzerman drew), he carried the puck into Vancouver's zone, chased it to the net, and wrapped it around and past Cloutier.

Something was going to end, if something didn't start. The Wings finally got started. And what should encourage them most is, they looked perfectly normal doing it.

Steve Yzerman guides the puck past the Canucks' Mattias Ohlund, giving the Red Wings a 3-2 lead early in the third period.

PHOTO: DAVID GURALNICK

Captain courage

Yzerman's winning goal shifts series momentum

BY TED KULFAN

For a guy supposedly playing on one good leg, Red Wings captain Steve Yzerman is putting every other player on the ice to shame.

Yzerman, playing with an injured right knee, again was the hero Tuesday night in a 4-2 victory over the Vancouver Canucks in Game 4 of a Western Conference quarterfinal series.

Red Wings	4
Canucks	2
Series tied, 2-2	

Yzerman, who also assisted on Chris Chelios' power-play goal, broke a 2-2 tie 56 seconds into the third period. Kris Draper added an empty-net goal with 53 seconds remaining.

The Wings won two straight in Vancouver to even the best-of-seven series at two games apiece. In so doing, they regained home-ice advantage as the series returns to Detroit for Game 5 on Thursday night at Joe Louis Arena.

"There's not a whole lot to say," said Yzerman, whose goal moved him past Gordie Howe and into first place on the Wings' career playoff scoring list with 159 points. "We realize we worked hard to get back in this series and let's not mess it up."

Canucks goalie Dan Cloutier was sprawled on the ice when Yzerman nudged the puck into the net while falling.

"He's playing unbelievable," Coach Scotty Bowman said. "He's playing hurt, but he's going to do it."

Jiri Fischer and Chelios gave the Wings a 2-0 lead in the first period.

45

1 Sergei Fedorov, center, started the Red Wings' first-period scoring burst at 4:02.

2 Mathieu Dandenault is congratulated after his shorthanded goal at 13:35.

PHOTO: JOHN T. GREILICK

3 Boyd Devereaux rejoices after scoring off a Brett Hull rebound at 15:32.

4 Sergei Fedorov watches his sweeping one-handed shot, after a fine pass from Brett Hull, elude Peter Skudra to cap the Wings' run at 18:31.

PHOTO: JOHN T. GREILICK

Fantastic Four

First-period scoring rush too much for Canucks; Fedorov gets three points

BY ANGELIQUE S. CHENGELIS

When Sergei Fedorov talks about playoff hockey, he talks about the nuances of a more honest, truer game.

He talks about the urgency of a seven-game series and the meaningfulness of every move and every pass.

Red Wings	**4**
Canucks	**0**
Wings lead, 3-2	

It is the type of pressure situation in which Fedorov, 32, said he thrives, and he proved that Thursday night with a two-goal, one-assist performance in the Red Wings' 4-0 victory over the Vancouver Canucks in Game 5 of a Western Conference quarterfinal series. The Wings scored all four goals in the first period.

Fedorov has three goals and three assists in this series, which the Wings lead three games to two. Game 6 is Saturday night in Vancouver.

"It seems to me in the playoffs it's easier mentally to come up for the games," said Fedorov, who played 26 shifts and took six of the Wings' 30 shots.

"You know what you're working for. It's not like an 82-game marathon. It's seven games you have in a series, and you need to get four wins.

"It's very reactable time. If you make a move or a pass or you make something good out there happen, everybody reacts. That way you've got a chance to make something happen."

Big Red is clicking now

Hull collects his first playoff hat trick in win

By Bob Wojnowski

Look out now. The big red reinforcements have arrived, and the Red Wings are rolling.

They bowled over Vancouver, 6-4, Saturday night, finally ending a first-round series that began in danger and ended with grim determination. The amazing part is, the fun is just beginning because the Wings are just starting to find their way around the ice.

Red Wings	6
Canucks	4
Wings win, 4-2	

Vancouver hung in as long as it could. It held off the first red wave, and the second. But by the time the Wings hit Game 6, more key players and elements were churning. The wealth and the goals were spreading, and the confidence was sprouting.

The strongest new wave? Brett Hull, who nailed his first career playoff hat trick. He had been a defensive stalwart but a scoring no-show. Not anymore. All three were classic Hull goals, sharp wrist shots, one short-handed, two on the power play.

Next wave? How about Kris Draper, the most-underrated player in the series. He drew penalties, he killed penalties and he made the play of the game. He raced past lumbering Ed Jovanovski to reach the puck, then was tripped into goalie Peter Skudra, sending him sprawling. With Skudra down, Nicklas Lidstrom flipped in the go-ahead goal, making it 3-2 in the second period.

Skate past, bowl over, whatever was needed. Igor Larionov was a puck-possessing whiz. Tomas Holmstrom scored a classic dirty goal. In wave after wave, the Wings

PHOTO: DAVID GURALNICK

Brett Hull and the Wings celebrate Hull's hat trick in the third period.

kept coming, sending young embattled goalie Dan Cloutier to the bench just 4:23 into the game.

Truth be told, this is the only formula that consistently works for the Wings. They can rely on Steve Yzerman, Sergei Fedorov and Brendan Shanahan for stretches. They can rely on goalie Dominik Hasek for periods. But they don't roll until they roll with everyone, and in four straight victories to close out the Canucks, everyone finally pitched in.

In the end, wacky GM Brian Burke was right. Vancouver was a little Canadian team desperately seeking an even playing field. By Game 6, the ice was tilting decidedly in one direction.

The biggest difference, obviously, was goaltending. If the Wings are lucky, they'll maintain that edge in every potential series the rest of the way. Well, every series but one. Of course, Colorado and Patrick Roy have to survive Los Angeles before we contemplate that matchup.

The Wings now await their next foe. Could be St. Louis, could be Los Angeles. Could be complacency. Could be rust.

You have to weather it all. Injuries. Goofy bounces. Goalie

48

Brett Hull beats Dan Cloutier from a difficult angle for his first goal.

roller coasters. Controversies and crises. That's playoff hockey. The Red Wings, postseason veterans for a decade, know it as well as anyone. One game, one period, you look horrible, incapable of advancing. The next game, the next period, you look unbeatable, incapable of losing again.

One minute, you're Hasek. The next minute, you're Cloutier.

One minute, you're a penalty-killer. The next minute, you're the ol' 600-goal scorer, Mr. Hull, again. His tallies were his first three of the playoffs, and that can't bode well for the Wings' next opponent.

"With this veteran team, there are so many guys, you're not always the one counted on, or the go-to guy," Hull said. "It's tough sometimes, but we've got enough guys that when someone is struggling, there's another guy to pick it up."

In every series, for every team, there's a random moment when it turns, and the stories align. For the Wings, it occurred with 25 seconds left in the second period of Game 3, a 1-1 tie, with Vancouver holding a 2-0 series lead. Lidstrom glided toward center ice and unleashed a slapper in the general direction of Cloutier, who bent slowly, too late to stop the puck.

Simple shot, slight bounce. The Wings won, 3-1, and Cloutier was never the same. At the other end, with the pressure shifted, Hasek started dominating.

Cloutier learned what the Wings know — it can turn at any moment. Playoff hockey is passionate and unpredictable, emotional mayhem. It's all about persevering.

Weather or wither, the oldest choice in the game. The Wings shook off trouble but it wasn't easy, and it won't get easier. The sign in the stands — "Official Drink of the Red Wings: Prune Juice" — tried to mock Detroit's age. But at the end of this series, age looked more like savvy. Hull looked spry again. And just like that, the Wings look doubly dangerous again.

Round 2, Wings vs. St. Louis

The beat goes on

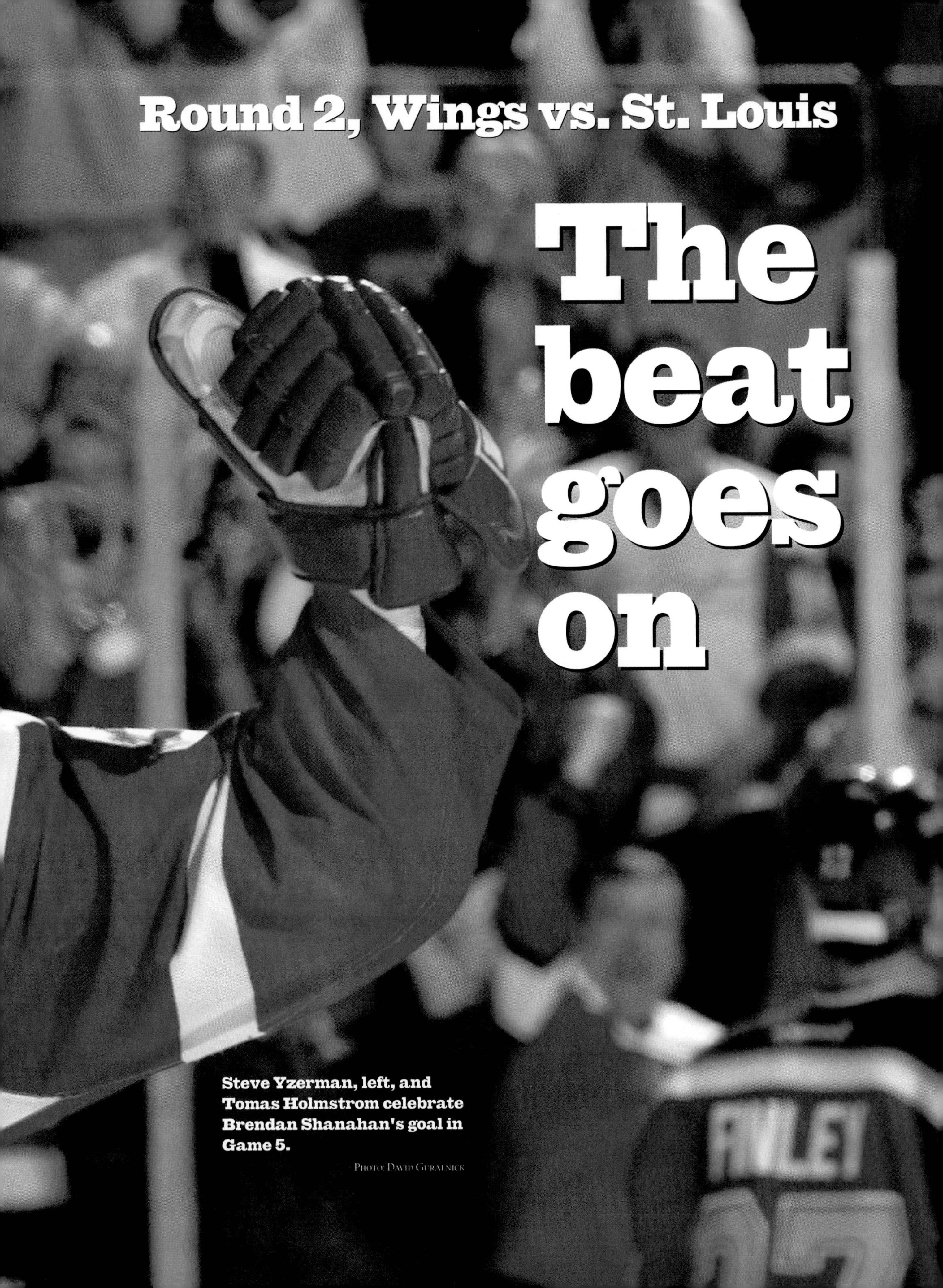

Steve Yzerman, left, and Tomas Holmstrom celebrate Brendan Shanahan's goal in Game 5.

Photo: David Guralnick

Brett Hull knocks his rebound past Blues goaltender Brent Johnson for a shorthanded goal in the second period.

PHOTO: DANIEL MEARS

Wings soar

Hasek makes 23 saves, Hull scores shorthanded goal to take series lead

By Ted Kulfan

This was the way the Red Wings wanted to open a playoff series.

The Wings' 2-0 victory over the St. Louis Blues on Thursday night in Game 1 of a Western Conference semi-final series was in stark contrast to an eye-opening loss to the Vancouver Canucks in the first round.

Red Wings	2
Blues	0
Wings lead, 1-0	

In the grand scheme of things, however, the Wings were far from pleased.

"I don't know if we played all that great," center Steve Yzerman said.

Maybe not, but goalie Dominik Hasek always was there to bail the Wings out.

Hasek made 23 saves for his second shutout of these playoffs and eighth of his career in the postseason.

Blues forwards Scott Young, Doug Weight and Pavol Demitra had glorious scoring chances turned aside by Hasek. "I was lucky, too. They hit three goalposts," Hasek said. "It was a very defensive-oriented game. My penalty-killers were very good in front of me."

Brett Hull had a shorthanded goal and assisted on Pavel Datsyuk's goal in the type of grinding, defensive-oriented game most everyone expected.

Datsyuk, returning after being benched the final two games against the Canucks, opened the scoring in the first period.

Hull's shorthanded goal, with 56 seconds to go in the second period, sunk the Blues. "Special teams are always a key in the playoffs," Hull said.

The Blues will seek to put more pressure on Hasek in Game 2 on Saturday. They thought Hasek got too many clean looks at the puck.

"Odds are if he sees it, he's going to stop it," Blues defenseman Chris Pronger said. "We need to battle harder in front of the net."

Chris Chelios and the Wings had plenty to celebrate after Brett Hull's shorthanded goal.

Photo: David Guralnick

Big 3 lead way

Hull and Robitaille score on power plays; Hasek holds off Blues

By Ted Kulfan

T hose big-name acquisitions Red Wings General Manager Ken Holland made in the off-season paid dividends nicely Saturday.

Goalie Dominik Hasek was the star of the game, and forwards Brett Hull and Luc Robitaille got power-play goals in a 3-2 victory over the St. Louis Blues in Game 2 of a best-of-seven Western Conference semifinal series.

Red Wings	3
Blues	2
Wings lead, 2-0	

The Wings have a two-games-to-none lead in the series, with Game 3 on Tuesday night in St. Louis.

Hull got his fifth goal of the playoffs and scored for the third straight game. Robitaille got his second goal and first in six games.

"On this team it doesn't matter who scores," said Robitaille, who got credit for the goal when a shot by Fredrik Olausson — another Holland off-season acquisition — deflected off his jersey.

"What matters is to get the win," Robitaille said. "We're happy to get the win, but we know St. Louis will come out strong in the next game. The third game is the most important of any series."

Steve Yzerman also scored for the Wings, giving them a

Brett Hull blasts a shot past the Blues' Brent Johnson for a goal in the first period, his fifth of the playoffs. The goal gave the Wings a 2-0 lead.

Photo: David Guralnick

1-0 lead on their first shot 2:46 into the game.

Scott Mellanby scored twice for the Blues. Mellanby scored 47 seconds into the third period and with 41 seconds remaining in the game after the Blues had pulled goalie Brent Johnson for an extra skater.

Mellanby's goals were the Blues' first against Hasek in this series. "He was superb," Coach Scotty Bowman said of Hasek. "On the (Blues' goals), he didn't have much of a chance. They were pressing. He made so many saves the first two periods."

Hasek finished with 35 saves and was at his best early in

54

the first period, when the Blues outshot the Wings, 9-1, over the first 10 minutes.

On a second-period power play, Hasek left Blues forward Keith Tkachuk shaking his head after a sprawling save.

"I was standing right there," Yzerman said. "It looked like a sure goal."

Hasek took the game in stride, stressing the importance of the Wings maintaining their momentum. They have won six straight playoff games since losing the first two of the first round against the Vancouver Canucks.

"We know that they (the Blues) will come out strong in St. Louis," Hasek said. "We know how fast things can change, just like they did against Vancouver."

The Wings were helped Saturday by taking the early lead. Johnson misplayed the puck behind the net, Sergei Fedorov pounced on it and made a quick pass to Yzerman in front.

Yzerman beat Johnson before Johnson was comfortably back in his net.

"It's easier to play with the lead," Hasek said. "Fortunately for us, it happened in both games here."

Blues fans littered the ice around Wings goalie Dominik Hasek with hats after Keith Tkachuk scored his third goal.

PHOTOS: DANIEL MEARS

"THEY DID A GOOD JOB OF SETTING SCREENS. I DON'T KNOW IF THEY DID ANYTHING DIFFERENTLY. THEY PLAYED A VERY GOOD GAME."

Dominik Hasek

Feeling blue

Bowman bemoans Wings' five penalties

BY TED KULFAN

Brendan Shanahan, left, Brett Hull, center, and Steve Yzerman talk strategy with Coach Scotty Bowman.

This time, it was the St. Louis Blues, not the Red Wings, who capitalized on their chances.

That translated into a 6-1 victory in Game 3 of a best-of-seven Western Conference semifinal series, cutting the Wings' lead to two games to one. Game 4 is Thursday night at the Savvis Center.

Blues	6
Red Wings	1
Wings lead, 2-1	

The Blues' victory also means the series will have a Game 5 on Saturday at Joe Louis Arena.

"I don't think they (the Blues) came out any differently," forward Steve Yzerman said. "They played very well. They capitalized on their power-play chances, and we didn't."

The Wings went 0-for-6 on the power play. The Blues went 2-for-5 — in the first two games in Detroit, they went 0-for-9. "We preach about it, but you can't take penalties," Coach Scotty Bowman said.

Keith Tkachuk had three goals, including one on a power play, for the Blues. Scott Mellanby (power play), Pavol Demitra (shorthanded) and Jamal Mayers also scored for the Blues. Pavel Datsyuk scored for the Wings.

After Demitra's goal, at 9:26 of the third period, Bowman replaced Dominik Hasek with Manny Legace.

"They did a good job of setting screens," Hasek said. "I don't know if they did anything differently. They played a very good game."

The Blues took a 1-0 lead on Tkachuk's goal at 5:41 of the first period. But the Wings roared back 27 seconds later on Datsyuk's goal. Bowman said forward Igor Larionov suffered a leg injury. It was too early to determine Larionov's status for Game 4.

Wings Notebook

NOT SO SPECIAL: Special teams were the hot topic for much of the first two games of the Red Wings-Blues conference semifinal series.

They will continue to dominate the headlines and airwaves for another few days.

The Blues, who couldn't get anything going on the power play through two games, were dominant on special teams Tuesday night in a 6-1 victory in Game 3. They went 2-for-5 with the man-advantage.

The Wings, who got two power-play goals to ignite their Game 2 victory Saturday, went 0-for-6 with the man-advantage Tuesday.

"The difference in the game," forward Steve Yzerman said.

ROAD WOES: Tuesday's result notwithstanding, the Wings are usually successful on the road. They had three road victories against Vancouver in the first round and 23 road victories during the regular season.

Before Game 3, several Wings said it's almost easier on the road.

"A team can relax and maybe not be worried about impressing the crowd," defenseman Steve Duchesne said. "You can concentrate on hockey and not have to worry about much else."

Dominik Hasek made 33 saves for his seventh victory of these playoffs.

Collision course

Blues enforcer Pronger out for playoffs with torn ACL

BY TED KULFAN

T he Red Wings are a game away from advancing to the Western Conference finals after a hard-hitting 4-3 victory over the St. Louis Blues on Thursday night.

If the Wings win Game 5 on Saturday afternoon at Joe Louis Arena, they can look back to one play midway through the first period of Game 4 that likely decided the best-of-seven series.

A collision between Steve Yzerman and Blues defenseman Chris Pronger left Pronger with a torn anterior cruciate ligament in his right knee. Although he played a short time after the injury, he did not return after getting called

Red Wings	4
Blues	3
Wings lead, 3-1	

PHOTO: DAVID GURALNICK

Brent Johnson reacts after his clearing pass hit Steve Yzerman and bounced into the net for a Wings goal.

PHOTOS: DANIEL MEARS

Steve Yzerman avoids a check by the Blues' Chris Pronger, who suffered a season-ending knee injury on the play.

for cross-checking at 10:20 and skating off the ice.

Blues General Manager Larry Pleau said Pronger will be out for the rest of the playoffs.

Yzerman said he was twisting to get out of the way when Pronger hit him in his rear end.

"He (Pronger) landed on his knee," Blues Coach Joel Quenneville said. "Those things happen. It's unfortunate."

Brendan Shanahan, Jiri Fischer, Tomas Holmstrom and Yzerman (power play) scored for the Wings.

"There's a big difference between being tied 2-2 or leading (a series) 3-1," defenseman Chris Chelios said. "This was a big win for us. Now we have to go back Saturday and win one more game."

Goalie Dominik Hasek had an outstanding game for the Wings, especially in the first half of the first period, when the Blues had three straight power plays.

The Wings were in control until Scott Mellanby and Keith Tkachuk scored for the Blues in the final three minutes with goalie Brent Johnson off for an extra attacker.

> ## "THERE'S A BIG DIFFERENCE BETWEEN BEING TIED 2-2 OR LEADING (A SERIES) 3-1. THIS WAS A BIG WIN FOR US."
> ### Chris Chelios

Halfway to Stanley

Hasek shuts out Blues, Shanahan scores twice

By Ted Kulfan

T he Red Wings are halfway to their ultimate goal.

The Wings defeated the St. Louis Blues, 4-0, Saturday to win the Western Conference semifinal series four games to one.

Brendan Shanahan had two goals and two assists, including one on Tomas Holmstrom's power-play goal, and Jiri Fischer scored. Dominik Hasek made 16 saves for his third shutout of the playoffs.

Red Wings	4
Blues	0
Wings win, 4-1	

"We had our best game of the playoffs," said Coach Scotty Bowman, whose Wings advanced to the conference finals for the first time since 1998.

The Wings will take on Colorado or San Jose in the conference finals. The Sharks defeated the Avs, 5-3, Saturday to take a three-games-to-two lead in that series. They play again Monday in San Jose.

"Whomever you face, you're going to play a hot team that's going to be sky high," Steve Yzerman said. "Either way, it's going to be a very difficult series."

The penalty-killing unit, which blanked the Blues on five power plays, was key.

"They weren't the same team as in early in the series," said Hasek of the Blues, who played without captain Chris Pronger (injured right knee). "You could tell they were missing Pronger."

60

Brendan Shanahan, who had one of his best games of the playoffs, celebrates the first of his two third-period goals.

PHOTO: DAVID GURALNICK

Red Wings center Steve Yzerman gets Avalanche goaltender Patrick Roy down on the ice during Game 6, but can't put the puck past him.

PHOTO: DAVID GURALNICK

Conference Finals:
Wings vs. Colorado
A classic

PHOTO: DAVID GURALNICK

The Red Wings' Darren McCarty flips the puck over Patrick Roy in the third period to complete his hat trick.

BY TED KULFAN

T he Red Wings always talk about unlikely heroes making timely plays.

Darren McCarty stepped into that role Saturday against the Avalanche in Game 1 of the Western Conference finals.

Red Wings 5
Avalanche 3
Wings lead, 1-0

McCarty, who had just five goals during the regular season, got three straight in the third period of a 5-3 victory.

McCarty's first goal, at 1:18, broke a 2-2 tie. He completed his first hat trick in 650 NHL games, regular season and playoffs. He had three goals at home in the regular season.

"I suppose when you score five in the regular season, and none in the playoffs, you're due," McCarty said.

McCarty became the second Red Wings player to get three goals in a period of a playoff game. Ted Lindsay got a hat trick in the second period against the Canadiens on April 5, 1955. McCarty became the seventh Red Wings player to get three points in a period of a playoff game.

"They were all great shots, too, they weren't garbage goals," Brendan Shanahan said.

"It's a wonderful effort from a guy who gives it his all every game," Coach Scotty Bowman said. "He's been a player that's done great things before."

Game 2 of the best-of-seven series is Monday night at Joe Louis Arena. Tomas Holmstrom (power play) and Brett Hull also scored for the Wings.

Joe Sakic (power play), Milan Hejduk and Alex Tanguay (power play) scored for the Avalanche.

"Their execution was much better than ours in the third period," Avalanche Coach Bob Hartley said.

McCarty's masterpiece

Grind-Liner shines with three goals in third period

Al Sobotka gets into the swing of things near Patrick Roy after a goal by Darren McCarty.

McCarty beat Patrick Roy from near the circles on the first two goals, at 1:18 and 12:41 of the third. He pounced on a rebound in front of the net to complete the hat trick.

"They were all great goals," Bowman said of McCarty's hat trick. "There wasn't anything lucky about them. You're doing it against one of the greatest goalies that ever played."

Bowman reunited the Grind Line of McCarty, Kris Draper and Kirk Maltby in the third period to thwart Joe Sakic of the Avalanche.

"We were looking for defense," Bowman said. "But that's how those things happen sometimes."

Certainly, McCarty's goals were crucial, but it was a goal by Hull that tied the score at 2 at 16:29 of the second peri-od. It was Hull's sixth goal and got the Wings back to even heading into the third period. With the Avalanche in the midst of a change, Roy made the initial stop on Pavel Datsyuk but couldn't get his glove on Hull's shot.

"We knew that line (Hull, Datsyuk and Boyd Devereaux) had practiced well all week," Bowman said. "They've created chances for themselves all season. That made a great play on the tying goal."

Hejduk gave the Avalanche a 2-1 lead at 13:36 of the second period. Hejduk's goal, his third of the playoffs, capped a three-on-two rush and apparently shifted the momentum toward the Avalanche.

The teams traded power-play goals in the first period.

Game 1 proves rivalry with Avs is as intense as ever

By Bob Wojnowski

Who says the rivalry has softened? Who? There was the reliable bruiser, Darren McCarty, pounding Colorado senseless and useless again, delivering shot after shot after shot.

OK. So he used his stick instead of his fists. And what he did Saturday goes to the top of the list of the Strange, Amazing and Ridiculous from hockey's greatest series. It's not just that McCarty scored three goals, all in the third period, shelling a shaky Patrick Roy and lifting the Wings to a 5-3 Game 1 victory.

It's that McCarty looked so, well, natural doing it. And the Wings, who like winning with stars but love winning with depth, looked so natural accepting it. And the poor Avs, who probably figured they'd buried the McCarty ghosts, looked a bit haunted. Uh-oh. Not that guy again?!

That guy again. It's just one game, and it's just three wicked shots, but when you're looking for positive signs for the Wings, McCarty is a good place to start. Actually, McCarty, who scored five goals the entire regular season and two in the previous three playoff seasons combined, thought he saw a different sign.

"You all read The Bible," he said. "You hear of the Apocalypse? There you go. Look out."

Look out, indeed. If McCarty is punching in, the Wings are punching someone out. And just like that, we have the first intriguing story line. The Wings saw everything that scares them about the Avs, who outskated them for long stretches. And the Avs saw the one thing that absolutely spooks them. Yeah, that guy.

Colorado likes it fast and pretty. That's why the Wings have to do it dirty, with a goal from Tomas Holmstrom, with a rebound from Brett Hull, with a hat trick from McCarty.

"Believe it or not, Mac has pretty good hands," Steve Yzerman said. "Of course, we may never see that again."

Of course, no one in the Wings' dressing room was willing to treat McCarty's breakout with a straight face. A note of caution for the Wings — someone else will have to pick up the scoring load because, for goodness sake, McCarty can't carry them forever.

How weird was it? Well, there was the interesting scene near the end, when Colorado enforcer Peter Forsberg sent a message to scoring star McCarty by plowing him over.

"Who knows why it happened," McCarty said of his feat. "I guess I was overdue. We talk about all the Hall of Famers, but what makes us successful is different guys chipping in. I guess this was my time to chip in."

It couldn't happen to a better guy, the team's dirty-work leader. It couldn't happen at a better time for the Wings, who weren't giddy with the way they played after a seven-day layoff. This is how it has to happen, if it's going to happen.

In 1997, McCarty pummeled the Avs' Claude Lemieux, then scored the overtime goal in that momentous victory. He added a game-winning beauty in the Cup-clincher against Philadelphia.

While the Avs rely heavily on the speed and brilliance of Forsberg and Joe Sakic, the Wings need their third- and fourth-line guys. They're the ones that have to make the Avs apoplectic, even if McCarty is being apocalyptic. They must keep doing it in Game 2 on Monday night.

If the world is still standing, that is.

Wings Notebook

GRIND LINE RETURNS: The Red Wings were looking for defense Saturday in Game 1 of the Western Conference finals. They were also hoping to contain Avalanche center Joe Sakic and his high-scoring line, and hoping to win some faceoffs.

Instead, the Red Wings got three goals from an unlikely source, and the defense Coach Scotty Bowman wanted, too. It resulted in a 5-3 victory over the Avalanche.

By reuniting the Grind Line of Kirk Maltby, Kris Draper and Darren McCarty, and going back to the Brendan Shanahan-Sergei Fedorov-Steve Yzerman unit, Bowman had the magic touch with his lines once again.

"We changed our lines because we couldn't put one line against them (the Sakic line) all the time," Bowman said. "We thought they were creating more as the game wore on."

Bowman said Yzerman's sore right knee was bothering him as the game progressed. He won only five of 17 faceoffs.

FIRST-ROUND WINNER: Wings goalie Dominik Hasek won Round 1 over his Avalanche counterpart, Patrick Roy.

Still, Hasek said, there's a long way to go.

"It's only one game," Hasek said. "I didn't think Patrick played a bad game. Darren (McCarty) made some great shots."

Lost chance

Drury scores winner as Avs even series

By Ted Kulfan

Chris Drury makes a move on Dominik Hasek before flipping the puck into a wide-open net at 2:17 of overtime.

Photo: John T. Greilick

The Colorado Avalanche got the split they were looking for. Now the pressure to produce is on the Red Wings.

Chris Drury scored at 2:17 of overtime to give the Avalanche a 4-3 victory over the Wings on Monday night in Game 2 of the Western Conference finals.

| Avalanche 4 |
| Red Wings 3 |
| Series tied, 1-1 |

The best-of-seven series is tied at a game apiece. The Avalanche, who swiped home-ice advantage away from the Wings, play host to Game 3 on Wednesday night. Drury rescued the Avalanche, who blew three one-goal leads.

"We got caught running around in our end, and he went to the net and scored," Wings captain Steve Yzerman said.

Drury scored after a nice pass from Steven Reinprecht on a play started by Peter Forsberg. Forsberg, shut out in Game 1, had a goal and three assists in Game 2.

"That line was great, they generated a lot," Avalanche Coach Bob Hartley said. "Peter is so creative and patient with the puck. That's what makes him such a special player."

"We have to play better defensively as a team," Wings defenseman Chris Chelios said.

"We played a bad game," goalie Dominik Hasek said. "We made so many mistakes. The way we played, myself included, we didn't deserve to win."

Red Wings goaltender Dominik Hasek doesn't let Dan Hinote distract him from making a save.

The Wings got two fluky goals on gifts from Avalanche goalie Patrick Roy.

Roy's misfired clearing pass led to a Kirk Maltby short-handed goal. Nicklas Lidstrom's power-play goal caromed off Roy's skate.

"We get to bail Patty out for once," Forsberg said. "He's always there for us."

> "I THOUGHT WE DID A LOT OF THINGS RIGHT, BUT WE DID LET ONE GET AWAY."
>
> **Brendan Shanahan**

70

Wings waste chance to put Avalanche, Roy on ropes

By Bob Wojnowski

When the Red Wings dissect this series, win or lose, this will be the game they'd love to have back. You get Colorado to the edge, you get Patrick Roy on his heels, you've got to push hard, and topple them.

The Wings let a gaping chance escape. It happens, especially against the defending champions. But you only get so many opportunities, and every one squandered makes the task that much tougher.

Colorado needed only one chance in overtime, on a pretty play by Chris Drury, to edge the Wings, 4-3, on Monday, knotting the series 1-1. This is how it will be, so get used to it. Punches. Counter punches. Goals. Counter goals. Mistakes. Punishment.

Colorado stayed a slight step ahead of the Wings, who committed the final mistakes, defensive lapses by Chris Chelios and Jiri Fischer that led to Drury's goal. The Wings had a chance to squeeze the Avs, playing better for stretches than they did in Game 1. They had Roy reeling again. They had their chances to bury him, but none of their big scorers could deliver the blow.

"I thought we did a lot of things right, but we did let one get away," Brendan Shanahan said. "They didn't have a lot of chances, but they don't need a lot of chances, similar to us. We knew this wasn't going to be easy. We're not hanging our heads."

The Wings shouldn't hang their heads. But they might consider kicking themselves. When Roy makes key mistakes, as he did, you've got to beat him.

Contrary to the billing, this has not been a goaltender showdown. This has been a scoring showdown, which should surprise (or alarm) absolutely no one. The Avs have held six one-goal leads in two games, and wasted all but one. This is the phrase you should clip and save, because it serves both teams: They just keep rushing.

Defensive hockey? Please. As much as players from both teams talked about playing tighter, you can't tether speed, and you can't soil skill. The Wings got burned last, and it didn't please their goaltender.

"We played a bad game," Dominik Hasek said, focusing on defensive miscues. "We didn't play well enough to win. We made so many mistakes."

This was about action and reaction, crimes and punishment. The Wings committed too many crimes (penalties), and no one punishes like the Avs.

Two games don't tell us everything. But they do present a couple budding story lines.

First, if the Wings keep taking penalties, they will lose. Simple as that. Colorado's power play is superb. The Avs' first goal, by Alex Tanguay, came precisely four seconds into the their first power play. It was their third power-play goal in two games and it should have frightened the Wings into prudence, but it didn't. Fischer took three consecutive penalties at one point.

The second story line is about speed. Colorado jumps into the rush better than any team in hockey. Other than Sergei Fedorov and Kris Draper, the Wings can't match the Avs' skating. The theory is, if the Wings' third- and fourth-line guys pitch in, they don't have to match the Avs' skating.

The goaltenders are good enough to cancel each other out. What it might come down to is this: Gliders versus goats and grinders.

Peter Forsberg, Joe Sakic, Tanguay? Those would be the Colorado gliders. Forsberg was tremendous, with four points.

Goats and grinders? Those would be Detroit's unusually productive secondary lines. Boyd Devereaux, member of the Two Kids and a Goat Line, scored. Kirk Maltby, the Grind Liner, scored on a gaffe by Roy, who came way out of the net to clear the puck and fired it to Maltby. These are the guys the Wings need now, at least until the big guns get unlimbered.

Wings Notebook

BEST OF ENEMIES: This is Maltby's fifth Wings-Avalanche playoff series.

"I won't say warm and fuzzy," Maltby said of the rivalry. "It's about respect. We know what each team is capable of doing. A lot of it gets blown out of proportion as far as the hatred and blood spill.

"I think players that were involved in that are gone, moved on to other teams. The ones that are still here want to go on to the next round. It's two very good teams trying to move on and win. There is respect there. I think there is a lot more respect there than there is any type of hatred or anything like that."

FIGHT AT FINISH: Chris Chelios and Avalanche defenseman Darius Kasparaitis got into a skirmish after Drury's winning goal.

Kasparaitis was penalized for elbowing at the end of the game.

Long time coming

Olausson's first playoff goal in 10 years lifts Wings in overtime

Brendan Shanahan and Fredrik Olausson celebrate Olausson's overtime goal that won Game 3 for the Red Wings.

Photo: David Guralnick

Stanley's Back!
Conference Finals, Game 3, Denver

By Ted Kulfan

Defenseman Fredrik Olausson, the unheralded free-agent acquisition in the off-season, scored at 12:44 of overtime to give the Red Wings a 2-1 victory over the Avalanche on Wednesday in Game 3 of the Western Conference finals.

Olausson took a pass from Steve Yzerman and blistered a shot from near the blue line that might have deflected off Avalanche defenseman Martin Skoula past goalie Patrick Roy. Roy barely moved on the shot.

| Red Wings 2 |
| Avalanche 1 |
| Wings lead, 2-1 |

"They were caught in a line change," Olausson said. "Patrick saw the shot. I got in a good spot."

It was Olausson's first playoff goal since April 18, 1992.

"I don't know if it's my most important goal," he said. "I haven't really thought about it. It's nice to get one."

The Wings' goal was fitting. They dominated the play during much of the game.

"This may have been our best game of the playoffs," said Luc Robitaille, who got the Wings' other goal. "A real strong forecheck, we created a lot of chances. It was a real good effort."

The Wings took a two-games-to-one lead in the best-of-seven series.

Robitaille scored his third goal of the playoffs, and first of this series, at 5:20 of the third period to tie the score. He was the closest to the puck after a shot from Sergei Fedorov went off the arm of Avalanche defenseman Greg de Vries, past Roy.

The only puck to beat Wings goalie Dominik Hasek was a power-play goal by Rob Blake at 15:54 of the first period.

"THIS MAY HAVE BEEN OUR BEST GAME OF THE PLAYOFFS. WE CREATED A LOT OF CHANCES. IT WAS A REAL GOOD EFFORT."
Luc Robitaille

73

Fredrik Olausson, the unheralded off-season free-agent acquisition who scored Game 3's winning goal, and goalie Dominik Hasek celebrate the victory.

PHOTO: DANIEL MEARS

Wings find success when they turn up heat on Avs

BY JOHN NIYO

Burning questions Wednesday after the Wings' 2-1 overtime victory over the Avalanche in Game 3 of the Western Conference finals:

Q. A victory is a victory, but the Wings deserved this one, didn't they?

A. "Can't play any better than that, can we?" associate coach Dave Lewis asked rhetorically as he headed for the team bus Wednesday night.

That's not entirely true, not with the Wings still having held the lead for fewer than 20 of the nearly 200 minutes in this series.

But it would be hard to argue in the afterglow of a game that could prove pivotal in this series. One thing is certain: A loss after outshooting the Avalanche by a 2-to-1 margin — the Wings had 42 shots to 21 for the Avalanche — would have been devastating for the Wings.

Q. Fine, then, what put the Wings over the top?

A. Patience, or a lack thereof, oddly enough. The Wings can't afford to sit back against the Avalanche, not with Peter Forsberg unleashed and Joe Sakic's line hunting scoring chances.

So, Scotty Bowman insisted this week — just as he did in the last series against St. Louis — that the best defense for his aging, veteran team would have to be an offense that applied pressure, and lots of it.

Bowman shuffled his forward lines to provide more balance, both offensively and in ice time. (No Wings forward played more than 20 minutes — or fewer than 12 — in regulation.)

And the defensemen joined the rush, early and often.

That paid dividends in the end, as Fredrik Olausson (six shots) scored the winning goal.

"I actually told the team, 'The way Carolina has been skating (in the Eastern Conference finals), that's what you've got to do,'" Bowman said. "You're not going to beat Colorado if you're not going to skate."

Q. Who skated best Wednesday?

A. Take a bow, Kris Draper. Ditto Kirk Maltby. The Grind Line was effective again in Game 3, helping Bowman roll four lines.

But the play of Jason Williams — he centered Steve Yzerman and Brendan Shanahan — was a big boost early. And shifting Sergei Fedorov to center Luc Robitaille and Tomas Holmstrom allowed Bowman the chance to give both wingers more ice time.

Still, the unsung hero might be Jiri Fischer, who jumped into the play smartly but not to the detriment of his defensive game. He finished with a game-high 12 hits.

Q. Speaking of Forsberg, where was he in this one?

A. Shadowed by another Swede, quite often. Give the Wings coaches credit for their in-series adjustments, and question Bob Hartley's decision to repeatedly send Forsberg's line out against Nicklas Lidstrom and Olausson.

In Game 2, Forsberg, Steve Reinprecht and Chris Drury ran circles around the Wings, who relied heavily on the defensive pairing of Chris Chelios and Fischer.

But for most of regulation Wednesday, it was a Swedish staredown, and the results were stifling, if not startling. No shots on goal for Forsberg, and none for Reinprecht. The line was a combined minus-5 for the night.

PHOTO: DANIEL MEARS

Luc Robitaille slips the puck past the Avalanche's Patrick Roy to tie the score in the third period.

Wings Notebook

NO LONGER OVERSHADOWED: Defenseman Fredrik Olausson always winds up as the other guy when the Wings' free-agent acquisitions are brought up.

Dominik Hasek, Luc Robitaille, Brett Hull, and, oh yes, Olausson.

That's not likely to happen much anymore. Olausson scored the winner at 12:44 of overtime Wednesday, giving the Wings a 2-1 victory over the Avalanche.

It was Olausson's first goal in the playoffs since April 18, 1992.

"It's been a long time," Olausson said. "It's nice to get one."

Olausson fired from the blue line, the puck deflecting off Avs defenseman Martin Skoula and past startled goaltender Patrick Roy.

"We caught them in a line change," said Olausson, who was signed to essentially replace defenseman Larry Murphy. "The puck may have hit their defenseman. It may have surprised Patrick a little bit. I'm happy it went in."

NEW LINES: Bowman, as expected, tinkered slightly with his forward lines.

Bowman inserted Sergei Fedorov between Luc Robitaille and Tomas Holmstrom, while putting youngster Jason Williams on a line with Steve Yzerman and Brendan Shanahan.

Bowman reunited the Grind Line of Kirk Maltby, Kris Draper and Darren McCarty, while keeping intact the Boyd Devereaux, Pavel Datsyuk, Brett Hull line.

"It seemed our lines were better," Bowman said.

PHOTO: DAVID GURALNICK

Avalanche goaltender Patrick Roy deflects a shot from Tomas Holmstrom in the first period.

Tracking trends

FREDRIK OLAUSSON got his fifth career playoff goal in Game 3. His previous four were with the Winnipeg Jets, who were 2-2 when Olausson had scored.

SERGEI FEDOROV has gone nine playoff games without a goal, the second-longest postseason streak of his career. He went 10 games without a goal in 1996.

The Red Wings have allowed eight power-play goals in their last six playoff games. They allowed just four power-play goals in their first eight playoff games.

Avalanche defenseman ROB BLAKE got his first power-play goal in these playoffs (17 games) in Game 3. He had 10 in 75 regular-season games.

The Avalanche's top two lines have accounted for six of their eight goals in the conference finals against the Wings. The other two were scored by defensemen. The Wings' top two lines have accounted for two of their 10 goals. Their third and fourth lines have combined for six goals; and defensemen have combined for two.

Michael Katz

76

Robitaille finds the net at most opportune time

BY TED KULFAN

It doesn't matter how the puck went in, forward Luc Robitaille was just pleased it did.

Robitaille didn't even touch the puck that glanced off the body of Avalanche defenseman Greg De Vries and past goaltender Patrick Roy on Wednesday.

"I'm just happy the puck went in, and we tied the score," said Robitaille, who was credited with the goal at 5:20 of the third period. "That was the most important thing."

As one of the key acquisitions during the off-season, Robitaille was one of the stars under pressure to produce in these playoffs.

That production has been sporadic at best. Wednesday's goal was only the third in the playoffs for Robitaille and his first in six games.

Robitaille, who saw his ice time diminish before playing 17 minutes, 3 seconds Wednesday, said he was disappointed with his production.

"You always want to help the team," Robitaille said. "But fortunately, the team was winning. That's the most important thing. We were winning."

Coach Scotty Bowman put Robitaille on a line with center Sergei Fedorov and wing Tomas Holmstrom on Wednesday. The move seemed to energize Robitaille, who played his best game.

"We had better balance on our lines," Bowman said.

Robitaille said the extra ice time helped, as did playing with Fedorov.

"He's such a great player," Robitaille said of Fedorov. "He creates so many chances out there. It was a big game by everyone. We had a big effort from the entire team."

"We played pretty forceful hockey and tried to put the puck on net, tried to get some traffic going," Fedorov said. "Some things worked for us; some things didn't. We pressed hard offensively.

"We could have had another one in overtime. We just work hard, I guess. We try to support each other on cycling the puck. Tomas likes to be around the net, and Luc is a good player one-on-one. I knew that somewhere there would be loose pucks. I kept cycling and between those two, things were happening."

> ## "YOU ALWAYS WANT TO HELP THE TEAM. BUT FORTUNATELY, THE TEAM WAS WINNING. THAT'S THE MOST IMPORTANT THING."
> ### Luc Robitaille

Luc Robitaille tries to get a shot on Avalanche goaltender Patrick Roy in the second period. Robitaille, who scored in the third period, had been feeling pressure to produce in the playoffs coming into Game 3.

PHOTO: DAVID GURALNICK

Avalanche warning

Sakic, Drury goals in third force Wings to settle for series split

By Ted Kulfan

The Red Wings dominated most of the two games at the Pepsi Center but are coming home with just a split.

The Wings controlled play through the first two periods of Game 4 on Saturday, but the Colorado Avalanche won the third, and the game, 3-2.

**Avalanche 3
Red Wings 2
Series tied, 2-2**

Avalanche forwards Joe Sakic and Chris Drury scored in the third period to break a 1-1 tie. Brett Hull completed the scoring with 2.7 seconds remaining, his team-best seventh goal of the playoffs.

The best-of-seven Western Conference finals series is tied at two games apiece. Game 5 is Monday at Joe Louis Arena. Game 6 is Wednesday at the Pepsi Center.

"The first two periods, we played very well," Wings captain Steve Yzerman said. "They scored right off the bat in the third period, and it energized them. They began to carry the play."

The final period easily was the Avalanche's best in the two games in Denver. The Wings had outshot the Avalanche, 25-12, through two periods. But the Avalanche outshot the Wings, 10-8, in the third.

The Avs' Dan Hinote, being shadowed by Chris Chelios, is stopped by Dominik Hasek on a first-period scoring chance. Hasek made 19 saves on 22 shots.

PHOTO: DAVID GURALNICK

79

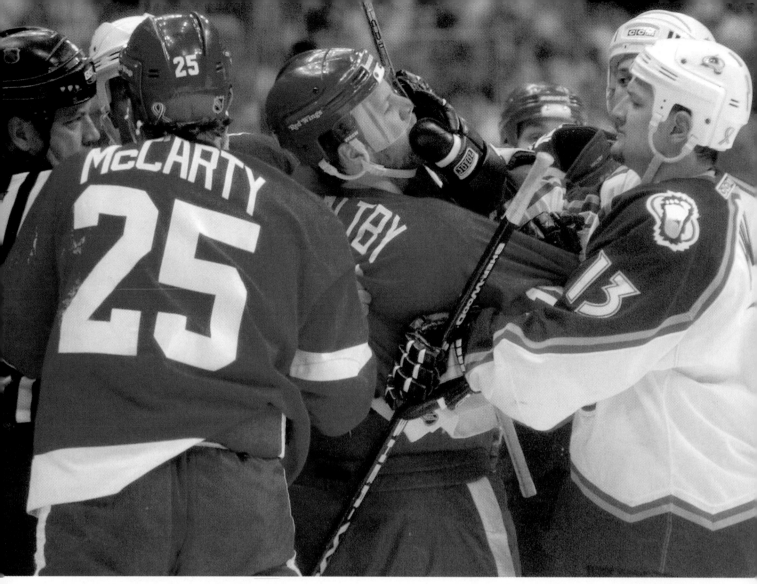

PHOTO: DAVID GURALNICK

The Avalanche's Dan Hinote, right, gives Kirk Maltby a taste of his glove in the second period.

"Through two periods it was the same as the other night," Sakic said. "We were happy with the way we finished. We found a way to win, and Patty (goalie Patrick Roy) gave us a chance to win."

Roy was outstanding for the second consecutive game, with 31 saves. Drury got his seventh career playoff goal — five of those have been winners.

This series was predicted to be long and entertaining, and it is turning out to be just that.

"It's disappointing because we had a lot of confidence after the second period," Wings goalie Dominik Hasek said. "Every game is a one-goal difference. One mistake and it's the difference in the game."

Sergei Fedorov (shorthanded) also scored for the Wings. Steven Reinprecht also scored for the Avalanche.

Sakic scored 45 seconds into the third period, his NHL-best ninth goal of these playoffs.

Avalanche defenseman Greg De Vries flipped a puck to Sakic, who caught the Wings on a bad line change.

Sakic beat Hasek with one of his familiar wrist shots, low and to the right.

"They had a lot more jump after that goal," Wings defenseman Nicklas Lidstrom said.

Each team went 0-for-5 on the power play. The Wings haven't scored in their last eight chances.

"It was the type of game where one power-play goal could have made a big difference," forward Brendan Shanahan said.

Fedorov made it 1-1 at 6:20 of the second period when he stripped the puck from Avalanche forward Peter Forsberg near the boards and went in on Roy on a breakaway.

Fedorov made a beautiful move to his backhand and slipped the puck through Roy's legs for the Wings' sixth shorthanded goal of these playoffs.

It was Fedorov's third goal of the playoffs and ended a nine-game scoring drought, the second-longest of his career.

The Wings outshot the Avalanche, 16-8, in the first period, playing just like they did in Game 3, when they outshot

Wings still figure to conquer Avalanche with depth

By John Niyo

Burning questions after the Red Wings' 3-2 loss to the Colorado Avalanche on Saturday in Game 4 of the Western Conference finals:

Q: The series is tied, but is it even?

A: Yes and no, quite honestly.

It is where it counts, thanks to Colorado's ability to get big goals in an instant from its top players.

Saturday, it was Joe Sakic and the NHL's most dangerous wrist shot that tripped up the Wings in the first minute of the third period. In Game 2, it was Peter Forsberg who stole the show. And in both victories, Chris Drury applied the finishing touch.

Still, the reason for Scotty Bowman's postgame nonchalance Saturday is his team's depth. That still figures to be decisive in this series, one that could, and probably should, go the seven-game distance. The Wings were dominant for the bulk of both games in Denver, rolling four lines and getting key contributions from each.

The Avalanche, meanwhile, haven't gotten a goal from their third or fourth lines in the series, and it stands to reason six forwards won't beat 12.

Q: That might be true, but didn't Colorado's coach shuffle his lines late in Game 4?

A: He did, in fact, and Bob Hartley has proven he's more than capable of matching wits, and lines, with Bowman, who gave the Wings an edge with his magic touch in Game 3.

Hartley broke up his top two lines in a move that was, perhaps, a bit overdue. He moved Dan Hinote and Eric Messier up to add a more physical element to the skill of players like Sakic and Forsberg, creating a better forecheck in the third period.

"And I don't think the Wings liked it," Hartley said.

Q: What was there to like in Saturday's loss?

A: The play of Sergei Fedorov, for one thing.

Fedorov, arguably the best player to this point in the series, finally got a goal Saturday to go with eight shots, double the total of any other player in the game. The goal ended a nine-game streak without one in the playoffs for Fedorov, the second-longest drought of his career.

But even without scoring, Fedorov has been dominant as a two-way player, backchecking well and creating chances regardless of his linemates.

Luc Robitaille's play — he's hampered by nagging injuries — continues to be a disappointment in the playoffs. Enough so, in fact, that getting Jason Williams back in the lineup must at least be a consideration.

Photo: David Guralnick

The Avs' Adam Foote, right, and the Wings' Luc Robitaille chase down the puck.

Q: Any other bright lights?

A: After Game 4, Bowman also was singing the praises of Pavel Datsyuk's line with Brett Hull and Boyd Devereaux. And rightly so: It has been the Wings' most consistent trio offensively in the playoffs.

But all the power-play time in Saturday's game, 20 minutes of scoreless hockey, actually worked in Colorado's favor, taking away even-strength ice time from Datsyuk's line.

Q: Speaking of the power play, what's wrong with the Wings' unit?

A: It's a question even the Wings' coaching staff is struggling with, trying to find different combinations that work without much luck.

Give Colorado it's due: Hartley's team uses an aggressive penalty kill and relies on Patrick Roy's superb positioning. But with Mike Keane out of the lineup Saturday, and the Wings winning two-thirds of their faceoffs, Detroit's power play should have generated more chances than it did.

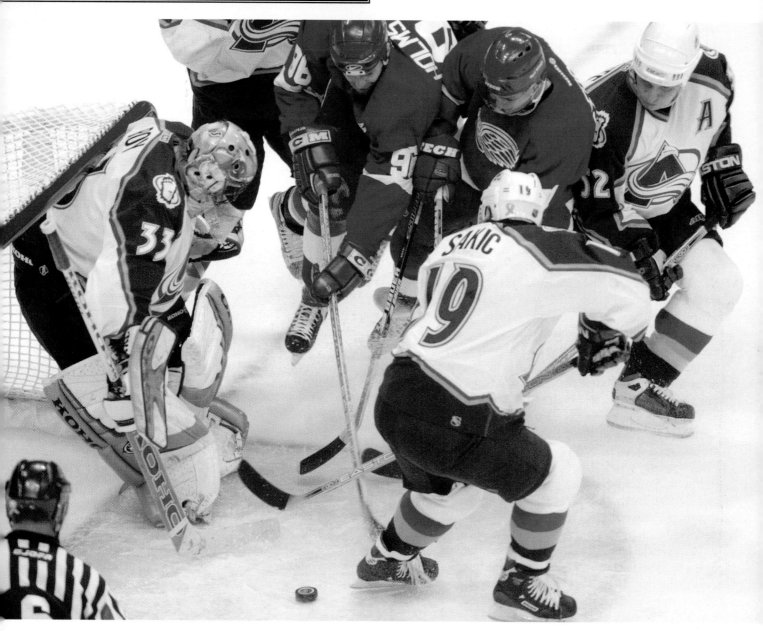

PHOTO: DAVID GURALNICK

Tomas Holmstrom, left, and Sergei Fedorov fail to get the puck past Colorado's Patrick Roy.

Tracking trends

■ The Red Wings' first and second lines have accounted for two goals and their third and fourth lines eight goals in the series against the Avalanche. The Avalanche's first and second lines have accounted for eight goals and their third and fourth lines no goals.

■ Avalanche goalie **PATRICK ROY** is 6-0 with a 1.33 goals-against average and a .952 save percentage in his last six starts in these play-offs following a loss. Overall in these playoffs, he is 7-1 with a 1.38 goals-against average.

■ The Red Wings went 0-for-5 on the power play in Game 4. In their last nine playoff games during the last two rounds, they are 6-for-40 (15 percent) with the man advantage. It is a stark contrast to the first round, when they went 7-for-25 (28 percent) against the Canucks.

Michael Katz

Roy stellar with 25 saves in goal for Avalanche

BY JOHN NIYO

Whether the Red Wings took their best shot — that's a point they'll readily debate — they did take 75 of them.

And Patrick Roy stopped 71 in two games at the Pepsi Center. Advantage, Avalanche?

Maybe, maybe not. But, clearly, Colorado arrives in Detroit with a series split in the Western Conference finals thanks largely to the play of its future Hall of Fame goaltender.

Roy's play very nearly rescued the Avalanche from their own lackluster play Wednesday in a Game 3 overtime loss. He stopped 40 of 42 shots, allowing only a goal that was punched into the net by his defenseman and an overtime winner that deflected off another defenseman's leg.

In Game 4 on Saturday, it was Roy again who was the difference at a time when his team trudged through the first two periods for the second consecutive game. Roy, playing in his NHL-record 237th playoff game, allowed only Sergei Fedorov's breakaway goal on 25 shots through the first 40 minutes.

"Patrick, again, gave us a chance to win," Coach Bob Hartley said. "And then in the third, we saw our best players be the best players out there."

Indeed, they were.

It was Joe Sakic's goal early in the third period — scored on his trademark wrist shot — that sparked the slumbering Avalanche. Then Peter Forsberg's picture-perfect saucer pass set up the winner at 16:43 of the third. The recipient was Chris Drury, who seemingly scores the big goal every time Colorado gets the better of Detroit in the playoffs.

At the other end, Roy was solid, if unspectacular all afternoon. That, too, seems to be a given for Colorado, at least when the team is facing playoff peril. Nothing flashy, just a nearly impenetrable wall. Roy has a save percentage of .913 in the series, outplaying Dominik Hasek, whose save percentage is .886 after four games.

"He made some good saves," Wings captain Steve Yzerman said of Roy. "But I don't know that we dominated that much to say that the goalie held them in it."

Still, that is essentially what Roy did. And it's what he has done so many times for the Avalanche that the team, at times, uses Roy as a crutch.

"Every night, I go out there and try to give my teammates a chance to win," said Roy, offering slightly more than the terse, one-word answers he gave after Game 3. "I thought we responded well in the third period today. Three or four guys stood up."

Left unsaid, of course, was this carefully inserted needle: Roy was one of those guys.

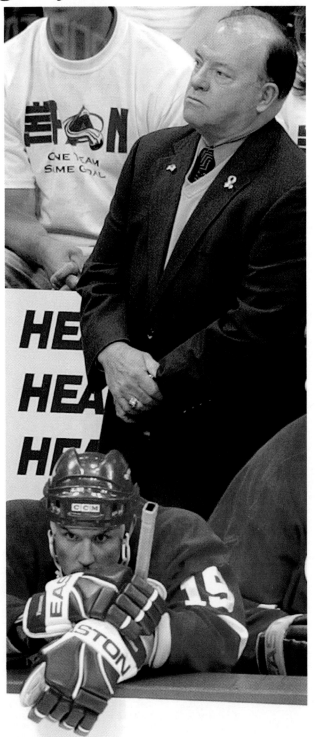

PHOTO: DANIEL MEARS

Wings Coach Scotty Bowman: "One team has to win two of the next three games."

BY TED KULFAN

eter Forsberg was denied in regulation but not in overtime.

Forsberg capitalized on a poor Red Wings line change at 6:24 of overtime to give the Colorado Avalanche a 2-1 victory in Game 5 of the Western Conference finals.

Avalanche	2
Red Wings	1
Avalanche lead, 3-2	

The Avalanche, the defending Stanley Cup champions, lead the best-of-seven series three games to two. They can advance to the Finals with a victory in Game 6 on Wednesday night.

The play leading to Forsberg's goal was close to being called offsides. It ended with Forsberg getting the puck alone in the neutral zone and beating Dominik Hasek.

"The puck started to roll after I made my first move, I was kind of surprised it went in," Forsberg said. "I'm not usually good on breakaways."

The Red Wings haven't won a game when facing elimination since 1996.

"There has to be a sense of desperation," forward Igor Larionov said. "You lose one more game, you lose the series."

Forsberg forces Wings into 3-2 series deficit

Backs against the wall

Peter Forsberg scores the deciding goal at 6:24 of overtime against the Wings' Dominik Hasek.

PHOTO: DANIEL MEARS

85

PHOTO: DANIEL MEARS

Brett Hull greets Steve Yzerman, who tied a record held by Gordie Howe with his 67th playoff goal.

**"I'LL HAVE NIGHTMARES
ABOUT THAT ONE TONIGHT.
I WAS SHOCKED IT DIDN'T GO IN.
I DON'T KNOW HOW IT
DIDN'T GO IN."**

Brendan Shanahan

Each team had outstanding chances to win late in regulation. Brendan Shanahan missed a glorious scoring opportunity with 1:35 remaining. He had Patrick Roy down and out of position, but his shot hit the left goalpost.

"I'll have nightmares about that one tonight," Shanahan said. "I was shocked it didn't go in. I don't know how it didn't go in."

Hasek then gave the Wings a chance to reach overtime with two fantastic stops on Forsberg in the final minute.

"The next game is like a Game 7 for us," Hasek said. "We have to play a smart game."

Wings must move forward after questionable call

By John Niyo

Burning questions Monday after the Red Wings' 2-1 overtime loss to the Avalanche in Game 5 of the Western Conference finals:

Q. Is it over?

A. Well, in the heat of the moment, the Wings were still arguing Game 5 shouldn't even be over yet.

The Wings believed Peter Forsberg's goal should have been nullified by an offsides call, as Brian Willsie, who inadvertently set up Forsberg's winner, looked to be a few feet over the blue line when he took a pass from Darius Kasparaitis.

But replays did show Willsie might have kept the play onside, though it's hard to tell if his skate was on the ice.

Muddying the waters was the fact that linesman Brian Murphy was a few feet off the line and unable to get the proper angle on the play.

"It's a tough call," said Red Wings Coach Scotty Bowman, who at first glance claimed Willsie was offsides. "I'm not going to cry over a call like that. Those are the breaks in the game."

Q. So the game is over, but what about the series?

A. There's still a game — or two — left, so the answer is a definite, "No."

The Wings have played well on the road and continue to show signs that they're wearing down the Avalanche. They created chance after chance in the third period and overtime — with the score tied, no less.

Among the reasons, perhaps? Bob Hartley is relying heavily on his top four defensemen to get by, with only half-time help — at most — from Martin Skoula.

Q. Didn't you forget someone back there?

A. Oh, yes. There's that fellow in net, Patrick Roy, too. All he allowed Monday was Steve Yzerman's trick-shot goal early in the third period, and barely that one. Roy has stopped 155 of 167 shots in five games, for a save percentage of .928, outplaying Dominik Hasek ever so slightly.

Q. You're being kind to Hasek, aren't you?

A. Roy has been better, no question. But to pin this series deficit on Hasek wouldn't be fair. The Wings are guilty of the kind of mistakes they insisted they couldn't afford in this series, the last and most egregious being the turnover and the line change that led to Forsberg's overtime silencer.

The entire series, the Wings have talked about controlling Colorado's speed through the neutral zone, knowing this is a team that must score on the rush to score at all, at times. And in each of the three losses, that speed has burned the Wings in critical situations.

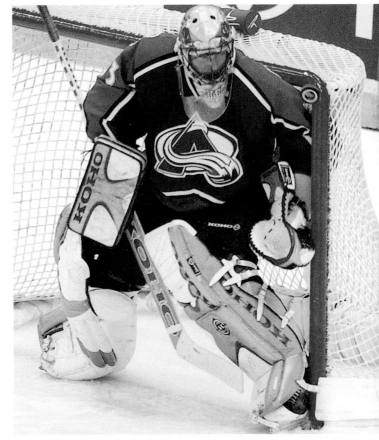

PHOTO: Daniel Mears

The Avalanche's Patrick Roy makes a save on a shot that lands on the top of the net.

What's more, it has been the tandem of Chris Chelios and Jiri Fischer victimized more often than not.

Q. Fine, but where have all the Wings' goal scorers gone?

A. That's the $64 million question, give or take a couple million bucks in the payroll department. The league's gaudiest roster — and the highest-paid bunch left in the playoffs — can't seem to find the net.

Yzerman tied Game 5 with the kind of crafty, veteran play we've come to expect from the Wings captain. But short of that, there's still the deafening silence from some of the Wings' star players up front.

Brendan Shanahan is still without a goal in this series, and that sound ringing in his ears today is no doubt the post he hit at the end of regulation. Meanwhile, Luc Robitaille's lone goal in this series came courtesy of a fluke bounce. He could use another fluke — and soon.

The Wings are, quite clearly, in dire straits.

87

Yzerman promises that series isn't over yet

By Dave Dye

Steve Yzerman's inspiration wasn't enough for the Red Wings.

The Wings lost 2-1 in overtime Monday night to Colorado in Game 5 of the Western Conference finals, but it wasn't because Yzerman didn't give everything he had to give once again.

Yzerman has played the entire playoffs on an ailing right knee that likely will require surgery during the off-season. He scored the Wings' only goal, at 54 seconds of the third period on the power play.

It was Yzerman's 67th career playoff goal, tying him with Gordie Howe for the most in Wings' history, and his sixth in these playoffs. Yzerman also leads the club with 170 games and 168 points in his playoff career.

Yzerman skated out from behind the net and from a horrible angle, shot the puck between Colorado goalie Patrick Roy's leg and the post. Few people realized the puck was in the net at first because Roy's leg was covering it.

But Yzerman started pointing at the net, and the referee responded by awarding him the goal. "I stepped out and banked it off the side of his leg," Yzerman said.

The record will mean more to him later on. On Monday, the focus was more on trailing three games to two in the series and having to bounce back for Game 6 Wednesday in Denver.

"I don't feel we're done or anything," Yzerman said. "Colorado played great tonight. It's our turn to respond with a big game in their building."

The Wings, who controlled the play for much of games 3 and 4 in Denver while gaining a split, got outshot, 9-5, in the first period Monday.

"We started poorly in the game," Yzerman said. "It was sluggish. We stuck with it and climbed back in it."

Both teams were slowed somewhat by the condition of the ice at Joe Louis Arena. The warm temperature outside had a negative effect on the surface. "The ice wasn't great," Yzerman said. "When the weather changes, it takes a while for the ice to adjust. It was slow, heavy ice."

The Wings have lost twice at home in the series, both in overtime. Colorado also won Game 2, 4-3, on Chris Drury's overtime goal. This time, Peter Forsberg scored the winner.

Yzerman disagrees with the perception that the Wings have been playing better on the road than at home.

"I wouldn't say that," Yzerman said. "I don't think we've

PHOTO: DAVID GURALNICK

Colorado's Darius Kasparaitis, left, and Steve Yzerman mix things up.

played much different in either building. We're an experienced team. Home or road, it doesn't matter to us."

Both teams are known for their offensive stars, but two of the last three games have been 2-1. "I'm not surprised by it at all," Yzerman said. "That's the style of hockey now. It's defense first. The top players have got to play well defensively.

"Colorado is a prime example that teams expect their offensive players to play defense first. It's counter attack. In '96, they played run-and-gun when they won the Cup. Now they play a patient game. They wait for their opportunities. You're forced to play that way, too."

Wings Notebook

GOAL IN QUESTION: Was the goal that put the Red Wings a game from elimination legal?

Many on the Wings believed that the play in which Avalanche forward Peter Forsberg scored in overtime could have been called offsides.

It wasn't, and the Avalanche won 2-1 in Game 5 on Monday night and head home with a three-games-to-two series lead.

Wings Coach Scotty Bowman said he thought the play was off-sides.

"You can't do anything about it," Bowman said, when asked if he was angry. "(Linesman Brian) Murphy wasn't on the line. You can't blame him. What are you going to do?"

Murphy and the rest of the officiating crew were unavailable for comment.

BOWMAN OPTIMISTIC: Bowman said the fact the Wings are 5-2 on the road in these playoffs gives him hope for Game 6 on Wednesday night.

"We have a good road record," Bowman said. "That's what you've got to take with you. And of the five games now, three went into over-time. It's been just about dead-even, but they got the goal to win the fifth game."

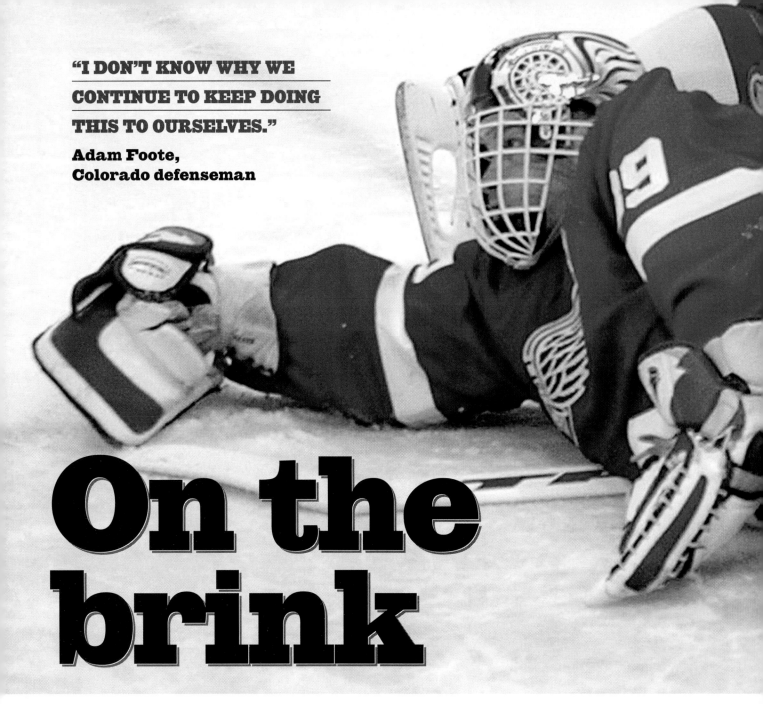

"I DON'T KNOW WHY WE CONTINUE TO KEEP DOING THIS TO OURSELVES."

**Adam Foote,
Colorado defenseman**

On the brink

With season in peril, Wings' goaltender makes 24 saves while Shanahan, McCarty score

BY TED KULFAN

Fittingly, there will be a Game 7 between the Red Wings and Avalanche in the Western Conference finals.

In a playoff series that will long be remembered as one of the best in NHL history, the Red Wings forced the deciding game with a 2-0 victory over the Avalanche on Wednesday night.

Goaltender Dominik Hasek made 24 saves for his fourth shutout of the playoffs, and Brendan Shanahan and Darren

Red Wings	2
Avalanche	0

Series tied, 3-3

Facing elimination, Dominik Hasek made 24 saves during his fourth shutout of the 2002 playoffs.

Photo: Daniel Mears

McCarty scored, helping the Wings stave off elimination.

Game 7 of the series is Friday night at Joe Louis Arena.

"We have home ice, and we have to take advantage of it," defenseman Chris Chelios said. "We have to take the same approach into that game that we did here."

For the first time in the series, the Wings scored first on Shanahan's goal late in the first period.

Playing with the lead, the Wings played as confidently and as well as they have the entire series.

"It's a different situation when you score the first goal," Hasek said. "It's a different situation when you play with the lead, and we played great defensively. We didn't give them much of anything."

The Avalanche, meanwhile, continued to lose players to injury. Already without forwards Mike Keane (ribs), Dan Hinote (broken left leg) and Alex Tanguay (ankle), the Avalanche lost forward Stephane Yelle (strained neck) on Wednesday night.

The Avalanche also are facing their third Game 7 of the playoffs.

"I don't know why we continue to keep doing this to ourselves," defenseman Adam Foote said.

Each team came out roaring early, putting aside any speculation on a conservative approach.

Patrick Roy and Hasek made big saves in the first 10 minutes. Hasek's best was turning aside an Eric Messier wraparound. Roy made a similar save on Boyd Devereaux.

"Both goalies have been very good in this series," Wings

PHOTO: DAVID GURALNICK

Fredrik Olausson roughs up the Avalanche's Peter Forsberg.

Coach Scotty Bowman said. "It takes a bounce to get any type of goal against either one of them."

Shanahan got his first goal of the series at 19:21 of the first period on the type of break Bowman said the Wings needed.

The Wings maintained control of the puck shortly after Roy made a tremendous save on Steve Yzerman from close range. Yzerman regained the control of the puck and fired a shot that Roy seemed to have controlled. Roy raised his glove, but he did not have control, and the puck trickled through the crease, where Shanahan poked it into the net.

Roy looked to be in disbelief that he didn't have the puck. He shook his head and buried it in his hands.

Shanahan had been looking to get on the scoreboard in this series, especially after missing an open net late in Game 5.

"I'm just glad we scored. We wanted to get the first goal," Shanahan said. "When you're a goal scorer, in the playoffs, it's not good enough to get chances. You want to put one in."

McCarty gave the Wings a 2-0 lead at 13:27 of the second period. It was McCarty's fourth goal of the playoffs, all in this series (he had a hat trick in Game 1). It also was his 20th career playoff goal, with seven coming against Roy.

"The second goal seemed to spur us on," Bowman said.

The Avalanche were on a power play late in the second period when their coach, Bob Hartley, challenged the width of Hasek's stick, hoping for a penalty on the Wings and a five-on-three advantage.

But the measurement proved Hasek's stick was legal and the Avalanche were called for a bench minor, nullifying the power play.

"I was surprised," Hasek said of the measurement. "I knew it was legal. I checked it before the game. They were looking for the two-man advantage on the power play."

Darren McCarty and Kris Draper celebrate after McCarty gave the Red Wings a 2-0 lead.

McCarty follows Game 1 hat trick with more heroics

BY JOHN NIYO

As blind squirrels go, Darren McCarty has simply gone nuts.

The Wings' rugged plowhorse did it again Wednesday night, beating Patrick Roy for a crucial goal — his fourth of the series — midway through Game 6 of the Western Conference finals at the Pepsi Center.

McCarty ripped a slap shot past Roy on the short side on a 2-on-1 breakaway to give the Wings a 2-0 lead at 13:27 of the second period.

For McCarty, whose hat trick in Game 1 in Detroit stunned Roy and the Avalanche, it was his 20th career play-off goal. Seven of those goals have come against Roy, widely considered the greatest playoff goaltender in NHL history.

Wednesday's goal was arguably the most important of McCarty's career, even more so than the magnificent Cup-winner he scored against Philadelphia in the 1997 Stanley Cup Finals.

"Every blind squirrel finds a nut," McCarty said after scoring that one. "I guess I found mine at the right time."

The time was right again Wednesday, with the Wings clinging to a 1-0 lead, the kind that hasn't lasted long in this series for either team.

That's when Jiri Fischer and Kirk Maltby helped start the 2-on-1 rush, with McCarty grabbing the loose puck, charging up the left wing and Maltby on the right.

"(Maltby) was joking about it later with me," said McCarty, who twice beat Roy with similar shots in Game 1. "He was my duck going to the net. He was my decoy."

For the Wings, it was only the second two-goal lead of the series, the last coming when McCarty was in the midst of a natural hat trick in the opener.

It was fitting, though, with Wednesday being the anniversary of the emotional flashpoint in this Detroit-Colorado rivalry: Claude Lemieux's controversial hit on Kris Draper in the 1996 conference finals.

The Red Wings' Tomas Holmstrom clears the Avalanche's Bryan Muir from the crease.

PHOTO: DAVID GURALNICK

History in Wings' favor going into Game 7 at home

By John Niyo

Burning questions Wednesday after the Red Wings' 2-0 victory over the Colorado Avalanche in Game 6 of the Western Conference finals:

Q. Alive, and well?

A. The Wings return home with renewed confidence, but don't believe for a moment that they think this series is in the bag, even with the injuries piling up for Colorado.

Still, here's the good news: NHL history says the home team is a 2-to-1 favorite in a Game 7, having won 66 of the 104 Game 7 situations since the best-of-seven format began in 1939.

But here's the bad news: No active player has more Game 7 experience than Patrick Roy (6-5 in 11 games). And Roy already has two Game 7 shutouts this spring — against Los Angeles and San Jose.

Q. Speaking of shutouts, was that Dominik Hasek's best game in a Wings uniform?

A. It certainly was his most important game, and perhaps this performance will quiet the critics who were ready to blame Hasek — unfairly so — had the Wings been eliminated here in Denver. Hasek's fourth shutout of these playoffs tied an NHL record, by the way. And he was clearly primed for this one, active and animated — as only Hasek can be — in net all night.

"That's why he gets paid the big bucks," Darren McCarty said, smiling. "That's his job, and he really relishes games like these — and it shows."

Q. Hasek withstood another challenge, too, didn't he?

A. Sure did. And he got the last laugh after Avalanche Coach Bob Hartley's lame attempt — desperation, perhaps?

— to get a five-on-three power play late in the second period.

Hartley called for a measurement of Hasek's stick blade at 17:37 of the second period with Colorado already on the power play. It was a move that immediately called to mind Marty McSorley's infamous illegal stick in the 1993 Stanley Cup Finals. Only this time, the blade was legal — no more than 3½ inches wide — and Colorado drew a bench minor.

Hartley, meanwhile, deserves ridicule for the move: A classless ploy — and a foolish one at that — in the midst of what has been a terrific, well-played series. On Wednesday night, Barry Melrose, the Kings' coach who was burned back in 1993, called it a "chicken" move by Hartley, with an expletive thrown in for good measure. Amen to that.

Q. But why would Hartley make the challenge if he didn't know the answer?

A. Hartley insisted after the game he had "information" that Hasek was using an illegal stick in the series. One possible source of the bad information? Hartley apparently requested one of Hasek's sticks from the Wings in the regular season as a souvenir for his teen-age son, who is a goaltender.

Q. Enough about the goalies — what about the skaters?

A. Scotty Bowman might have found the star quality he was searching for earlier in the series. Sergei Fedorov was brilliant again in Game 6.

Q. Anyone else?

A. Tomas Holmstrom might have had his best game of the series, while the Grind Line continues to impress. On the blue line, Nicklas Lidstrom played 30 minutes and helped nullify Peter Forsberg, who had only one shot on goal. And hard as it is to believe, Lidstrom has now played 17 games in the playoffs without taking a penalty.

Wings Notebook

HOME, SWEET HOME: All the Red Wings wanted to get one more game, one more opportunity.

They got both after defeating the Colorado Avalanche, 2-0, Wednesday night in Game 6.

The Wings forced a Game 7 at Joe Louis Arena, with the winner advancing to the Stanley Cup Finals against the Carolina Hurricanes.

"We've set ourselves for a Game 7," said forward Darren McCarty, who got his team-best fourth goal of the series.

"This series is far from over," McCarty said. "But we did what we had to do tonight, and that's play a real solid road game. We have to relish this opportunity."

GETTING THE LEAD: There was a lot of talk about the Avalanche scoring first in each of the five previous games in this series, forcing the Wings to rally.

The Wings finally got the first goal when Shanahan scored at 19:21 of the first period, pouncing on a puck that had eluded Roy.

Bowman thought the puck was under Roy's glove.

"I had no idea," Bowman said. "I thought he (Roy) had it in his glove, and I was a little disappointed. I thought that was probably our best chance we had to score trying to get the first goal in all the other five games."

Wings captain Steve Yzerman displays the Western Conference championship trophy.

7-Oh!

Wings bury arch-rival with four-goal avalanche in first period, advance to Stanley Cup Finals

By Bob Wojnowski

Nope. Not gonna do it. Sorry, but I won't. I will not ignore the evidence for the sake of being fair, or safe.

I will not sit here and deny my expertly trained eyes and tell you why the Carolina Whalers, er, Panthers, er, Hurricanes, could pull the shocking upset in the Stanley Cup Formality, er, Finals.

If I'm a fool, then I'm a proud fool, willing to dismiss conventional sports wisdom by stating the obvious. Now that the Red Wings have exploded the myth of Patrick Roy's Game 7 invincibility, all that remains is the rubber-stamping.

Ready? The Wings will win the Cup, their third in six seasons. They'll win it in five games. They'll win it easily because ... ouch! ... hey ... back off, Chelios! ... ow, ow.

> **Red Wings 7**
> **Avalanche 0**
> **Wings win, 4-3**

OK. So it's not the wisest thing to say around the Wings dressing room. I'm forced to say it because the Wings can't, or won't, or shouldn't. But really, who's kidding whom? The Wings were the NHL's best team in the regular season, by far. They just vanquished the defending champs in a 7-0 scrimmage. They have at least one Hall of Famer for every Carolina player you can name.

It's a mismatch, Hockeytown versus Tobaccotown. Down in Raleigh, more people are interested in raising the spit cup than the Stanley Cup. I'm not saying they're unfamiliar with hockey. I'm just saying they consider the Original Six to be the day's first six-pack.

Look at this objectively. The Hurricanes won 35 of 82 regular-season games. If you seeded the playoff teams one through 16, they'd be 15th. Their leading goal-scorer is some young center named Jeff O'Neill, well-known in certain areas of Raleigh. Their points leader, 39-year-old Ron Francis, is so old, he's a contemporary of several Wings.

I pose the question: When was the last time a professional team entered its championship round as such a huge underdog and emerged victorious?

"You ever hear of New England?" said the Wings' Chris Chelios, displaying his football knowledge, and his irritation. "Doesn't that show we've got to play our best? Carolina is a big, physical team. By knocking off Colorado, that should give us some confidence going into this series."

Excuse me? The Wings are the team seeking confidence? That's not what the experts (like me) say.

"That's why you guys aren't experts," Brett Hull snapped. "Me and Stevie (Yzerman) watched a lot of Carolina's games together. That team is young and fast and strong and very disciplined. We can't let anyone tell us it's over because they think we're so great. I don't think you guys take Carolina as seriously as you should."

Please. Wings goalie Dominik Hasek is on his way to supplanting Roy as the game's best. Carolina's Arturs Irbe is a simple journeyman. Sure, his .947 save percentage leads all playoff goalies, but when was the last time he ever got this hot? Um, other than 1994, when he led eighth-seeded San Jose to its first-round stunner over top-seeded Detroit.

Oops. Time to scramble for more information. I broke down every statistic, including the key one, payroll. Wings — $65 million. Carolina — $33 million. I even asked a respected NHL analyst, who shall remain nameless, for his view on the last time the Stanley Cup Final appeared this lopsided. He mulled it briefly.

"I'd probably say 1995," he said. "Detroit-New Jersey."

Oops. That was the series in which the unbeatable

PHOTO: ALAN LESSIG

The Red Wings celebrate Friday's first goal, scored by Tomas Holmstrom, right.

Wings were swept by the neutral-zone-trapping Devils.

All right. So maybe the Hurricanes have a chance, a teensy-weensy chance, because hockey is a sport of odd bounces and because New England beat the Rams. They do have some strange Southern charm working, including their hokey-hockey use of cheerleaders to rile one of the league's noisiest crowds.

Their coach, Maurice Paul (or perhaps, Paul Maurice), is a fuzzy-cheeked 35-year-old who surely gets carded when he tries to purchase an Original Six. He has lived almost as long as Scotty Bowman has coached (30 years).

You can see why it's hard to accept Carolina as a legitimate challenger, no matter how many Wings declare it so. One of Carolina's veteran leaders is a defenseman named Aaron Ward. Intelligent. Feisty. Tough. Perhaps you've heard of him. He used to be one of the Wings' least-appreciated players.

The disparities run deep, and high. Hurricanes owner Peter Karmanos Jr. so badly wants to match Mike Ilitch, he tried to swipe Sergei Fedorov a few years ago. He even has a player named Jeff Daniels to match actor Jeff Daniels, the big Wings fan.

> ## "YOU'RE GONNA REALIZE PRETTY QUICKLY HOW GOOD THEY ARE."
> ### Steve Yzerman

The Hurricanes might be hot, upsetting New Jersey, Montreal and Toronto. But are they any good? Before this season, the franchise was 1-11 in playoff series, dating to the glory years back in Hartford.

In these playoffs, they're 6-1 in overtime, suggesting some good fortune. After surviving Peter Forsberg and Joe Sakic, should the Wings really be frightened of Bates Battaglia (a Carolina player, reportedly)?

"They're well-coached and their goalie is hot," Yzerman said. "They're playing hungry, and they've got something special going on. That makes them really dangerous. You're gonna realize pretty quickly how good they are."

The Captain spoke sternly, like he wasn't kidding. Good. We do the kidding. They do the playing. And the Wings, who have been stunned a few times in the playoffs, swear they're taking nothing for granted.

That's the way it should be. And this is the way it will be. The Wings can't lose this series. They just can't, not in my expert opinion. I absolutely refuse to budge on this. Nope. Not gonna do it, not even after Irbe makes 47 saves and steals Game 1.

Theoretically, of course.

Hasek has one final goal to accomplish

BY ANGELIQUE S. CHENGELIS

Dominik Hasek had just seen the Red Wings preserve a 7-0 victory in Game 7 of the series with Colorado to advance to the Stanley Cup Finals. He had been the recipient of a standing ovation in a packed Joe Louis Arena on Friday night. He became the first NHL goalie to earn five shutouts in one playoffs.

But Hasek, the greatest goalie never to win a Stanley Cup, deflected talk of records. This was the time to discuss goals — not the kind he did not allow the Avalanche in the deciding game, but the kind that define a player's career.

"It doesn't mean anything," Hasek said of the shutout record. "It's nice, but I have a different goal, and it's not about shutouts.

"All I want to think is to get ready for the next game. It's far from being over. It's still unfinished business. We still have to win four games. I just feel we made a next step to the goal, what we are here for and win four more games."

The four-more-games refrain became a familiar one for the 37-year-old Czech after Friday night's rout, in which he made 19 saves. Hasek knows he is too close to his goal of winning his first Stanley Cup to be anything but focused on the upcoming Finals that begin Tuesday against the Carolina Hurricanes in Joe Louis Arena.

That Hasek has not yet won the coveted Cup seems remarkable, considering his vast array of accomplishments and trophies. He is a two-time NHL most valuable player, with Buffalo in 1997 and 1998, he is a six-time Vezina Trophy winner, and he led the Czech Republic to an Olympic gold at the Nagano Games in 1998.

Hasek came close to Stanley Cup glory in 1999 after leading the Sabres to the Finals. But Buffalo lost in overtime of Game 6 when Hasek's current teammate, Brett Hull, scored to give the Dallas Stars the victory. Hasek came to Detroit last summer for $8 million and a legitimate shot at the Cup that is now four victories away.

"I'm glad to be part of this great, great team, to be ready for the Finals," Hasek said. "I'm glad we won the first 12 games, but it's still a long way to go. Our goal was, and is, to win four more games."

His teammates are more than aware what winning the Cup would mean for Hasek. They played to preserve the shutout Friday night. They played to win not only for themselves, but to put Hasek in position to try again for

PHOTO: DANIEL MEARS

Goalie Dominik Hasek makes a save in front of the Avalanche's Alex Tanguay.

that elusive Stanley Cup.

"We were playing our hearts out for Dom," Kris Draper said. "He was unbelievable in this series for us, he's been great for us in the playoffs. When you go as far as you have, and he's working on a shutout in Game 7, you want to do everything you can to make sure that happens."

Hasek said he did not start to feel comfortable until the Wings had a five-goal advantage. He felt even more comfortable, he said, after Avalanche goalie Patrick Roy was pulled 6:28 into the second period.

"I wasn't sure if it was for me or for everybody," Hasek said. "It was a good feeling. What can I say? I felt happy to be up 6-0 with five minutes left, you feel like you could not lose that game. But I tried to be sharp until the very end. We still have to do our job. Of course I would like to hear (the ovation) again, but we have to win."

PHOTO: DAVID GURALNICK

Brendan Shanahan and Sergei Fedorov celebrate a first-period goal in Game 7 against the Avalanche.

Wings' depth was too much for Avs to overcome

BY JOHN NIYO

Burning questions Friday after the Wings' 7-0 victory over the Colorado Avalanche in Game 7 of the Western Conference finals:

Q. So what got into the Wings, anyway?

A. No one saw a rout of those proportions coming, but many who watched Game 6 closely could see the signs that Colorado was ready to collapse.

The Wings' depth, as predicted, proved to be the difference in the series, an advantage that was only exacerbated by Colorado's mounting injuries. Mike Keane tried to play despite a painful rib injury in Game 7, as did Alex Tanguay with a severe charley horse that might require surgery. Two other forwards — Stephane Yelle and Dan Hinote — couldn't go.

"Obviously, Colorado was a banged-up team — we knew that," said Wings Coach Scotty Bowman, who rolled four lines and used six defensemen. "And we knew that if we kept doing that we would probably have an advantage."

Q. Still, somebody must've said something to inspire a performance like that, no?

A. Believe it or not, before Friday night's Game 7, it was Bowman telling a few jokes in the dressing room that helped lighten the mood and relax the team.

"I just told them before the game a few stories about Game 7s that I'd been involved in," Bowman said. "And I told them that no matter what happens, it will be memorable — that I remember every one of them, whether we won or lost."

One could argue, however, that it was Dominik Hasek's sharp words after Game 5 that turned the tide in the series. Hasek ripped into his teammates for, among other things, the defensive breakdowns that let Peter Forsberg's line loose for winning goals in consecutive games.

"He's the goalie," Sergei Fedorov said. "And we have to do what he says, because he has to feel comfortable with the way we play. We want to have him in charge, and I think he likes that — that's why he did what he did."

Q. Now what will he do for an encore?

A. Don't expect a letdown, not with Hasek on the verge of the one award that has eluded him in his career. Hasek's five shutouts in the postseason are an NHL playoff record, but the Wings' goalie might have another one or two shutouts left in him.

Q. What about the other goalie in the Stanley Cup Finals?

A. One thing is almost certain: For the first time in NHL history, a European goaltender will carry his team to the Stanley Cup.

Never before have two European goalies met in the Finals, but Hasek's goaltending foe beginning Tuesday is Arturs Irbe, a 35-year-old Latvian whose name Wings fans no doubt remember. Irbe was in net when San Jose upset the top-seeded Wings in the first round of the 1994 playoffs, Bowman's first in Detroit.

Q. Can he pull off the upset again?

A. Probably not, at least not with the Wings playing the way they are coming into the series.

But Irbe could, at least, make things interesting. Bolstered by Carolina's tight, defensive style, Irbe has a playoff-best 1.41 goals-against average and a .947 save percentage. As ESPN's Darren Pang said after Friday night's game: "Arturs Irbe will decide whether this is a series or not."

What's the deal?

Sergei Fedorov's current contract was essentially written by the Carolina Hurricanes' management. Fedorov was a restricted free agent without a contract in February 1998, practicing with the Plymouth Whalers, Hurricanes owner Peter Karmanos' junior hockey team, in preparation for the Winter Olympics in Nagano. It was in Japan during the Olympics when he signed an offer sheet with Carolina.

The six-year, $38-million deal included a base salary of $2 million annually, a $14-million signing bonus and another $12-million bonus that kicked in if Fedorov's team advanced to the conference finals. That last bonus outraged Wings management, as the Hurricanes were a team that eventually missed the playoffs altogether. The Wings, meanwhile, were the defending Stanley Cup champions.

But the offer sheet was deemed valid by an arbitrator after the NHL filed a grievance over the bonus clause.

Wings owner Mike Ilitch quickly decided to match Carolina's offer rather than accept the NHL compensation of five first-round draft picks. When Fedorov returned to help lead the Wings to another championship, he received $28 million for 21 regular-season games and 22 playoff games.

Stanley Cup Finals: Wings vs. Carolina

One for the ages

Visions of the Stanley Cup were dancing on the Joe Louis Arena ice before Game 1 of the Finals.

PHOTO: DANIEL MEARS

SHOCKER!

Brett Hull can't slide the puck past the Hurricanes' Arturs Irbe.

Photo: Daniel Mears

Hurricanes shut down late Wings power play, Francis scores in overtime

Photo: Daniel Mears

Wings goalie Dominik Hasek leaves the ice as the Hurricanes celebrate their victory.

Fedorov, Maltby score as Red Wings come up short

By Ted Kulfan

The Red Wings were right. The Carolina Hurricanes are a lot better than people think.

Center Ron Francis scored 58 seconds into overtime, just after the Hurricanes killed off a Wings power play, for a 3-2 victory in Game 1 of the Stanley Cup Finals on Tuesday night at Joe Louis Arena.

Francis was wide open in front of the net after goaltender Dominik Hasek missed on a poke-check attempt. Francis flipped the puck past Hasek for his sixth goal of the playoffs.

"They didn't win tonight because they were lucky," Hasek said. "They won because they were the better team."

Game 2 of the best-of-seven series is Thursday night at Joe

Hurricanes	3
Red Wings	2
Hurricanes lead, 1-0	

PHOTO: ALAN LESSIG

Ron Francis sends the winning goal past the Wings' Dominik Hasek, who stopped 23 shots.

Louis Arena. The Hurricanes improved to 7-1 in overtime in these playoffs. The Wings dropped to 1-4 and saw their eight-game winning streak in the Finals come to a screeching halt.

"We'll take it in this series," Hurricanes Coach Paul Maurice said of his team's overtime success. "Obviously, we're comfortable there and we have had some great success."

The Wings had a great opportunity to end it in regulation. They were on a power play when Hurricanes forward Erik Cole was called for hooking Pavel Datsyuk at 18:19 of the third period.

But the Wings were unable to get anything going on a power play that extended into the first few seconds of the overtime.

"We had a chance to win it on the power play," Coach Scotty Bowman said. "That's just like being in sudden-death overtime. We didn't play as well as we wanted to."

Sergei Fedorov (power play) and Kirk Maltby scored for the Wings. "We're not shocked (with the loss)," Wings captain Steve Yzerman said. "Having watched them (Carolina) since the second round of the playoffs, they have a special thing going right now."

Sean Hill (power play) and Jeff O'Neill also scored for the Hurricanes.

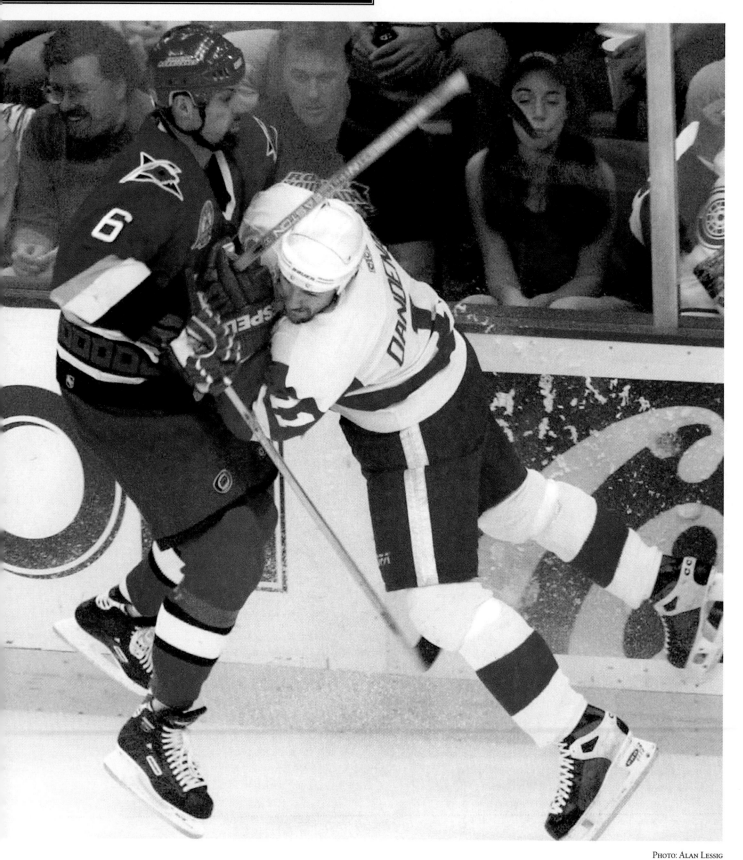

Wings defenseman Mathieu Dandenault puts a hit on Hurricanes defenseman Bret Hedican.

Potent power play is silent against Carolina

By Joanne C. Gerstner

Nobody can say the chances weren't there.

The Red Wings, the NHL's second-most successful power-play team during the regular season, had seven power plays in Game 1 of the Stanley Cup Finals.

Yet, only one goal was produced from those opportunities. And a 3-2 overtime loss.

"We couldn't take advantage of those opportunities," Wings left winger Luc Robitaille said. "We had chances. We knew they were a good team."

But the Wings also were strong in killing off five power plays, letting Carolina score once.

"I thought the officials did a good job," Hurricanes captain Ron Francis said. "From our standpoint, we did not want to take that many penalties against a team like that.

"Win or lose, both team had opportunities. Our penalty-killers did a great job."

The Wings were on the power play for 10:22, and the Hurricanes had 9:27 of advantage.

Sergei Fedorov scored the first goal of the game on a power play at 15:21 in the first period.

Carolina answered back with its own power play goal from Sean Hill at 3:30 in the second to tie the game 2-2.

"You can analyze it any way you want," Wings Coach Scotty Bowman said. "We had a chance to win it on the power play. I didn't think we played as well as we wanted to."

Both teams can likely look for more of the same tight officiating in Game 2 on Thursday at Joe Louis Arena.

"It was called very, very, very tight," Hurricanes Coach

PHOTO: DANIEL MEARS

Nicklas Lidstrom and Steve Yzerman congratulate Wings teammate Sergei Fedorov on his first-period goal.

Paul Maurice said. "We were aware from the conference call (Monday) that the standard was going to be held high in this series.

"Hopefully both teams will be able to adjust."

Maurice added: "We didn't take a lot of penalties during the regular season and we took more (Tuesday) than I would have hoped, no question. We will address that, but we have to play a physical enough game that we are involved."

Wings Notebook

POWER OUTAGE: One area where the Red Wings need to improve in Game 2 is the power play.

The Wings hardly mounted an attack, going 1-for-6 Tuesday night during 10 minutes, 22 seconds with a man advantage. The worst was a power play that stretched from the end of regulation into overtime, when a goal would have won it for the Wings.

Instead, the Wings lost 3-2 to the Carolina Hurricanes in the opener of the Stanley Cup Finals.

"You can analyze it any way you want. We had a chance to win it on the power play," Wings Coach Scotty Bowman said. "That's just like being in sudden death."

The Wings scored one power-play goal, by Sergei Fedorov to open the scoring. But the attack went

silent after that.

SPORTSCENTER MOMENTS: The Red Wings were represented well in nominations for the ESPY awards, which ESPN announced Tuesday.

Defenseman Nicklas Lidstrom and goalie Dominik Hasek were both nominated for best NHL player.

Ted Kulfan, Tom Markowski

Nicklas Lidstrom watches as Dominik Hasek knocks the puck out of the net after Carolina's Jeff O'Neill scored.

PHOTO: DANIEL MEARS

Tracking trends

■ The Red Wings have won just one of 10 Finals series in which they lost Game 1 since the best-of-seven format began in 1939. Four of those series in which they lost ended in sweeps.

■ The Hurricanes have won seven overtime games in these playoffs, the second-most in NHL history in one playoff year. The Canadiens won 10 on the way to the Stanley Cup in 1986.

■ The Red Wings dropped to 9-2 in these playoffs when scoring first. The Hurricanes improved to 4-5 in the playoffs when their opponent scored first.

■ The Hurricanes have outscored their opponents, 22-9, in the third period and overtime of these playoffs.

■ The Hurricanes won for just the second time in seven games in these playoffs when trailing after the first period. The Wings are now 8-2.

Michael Katz

Fans should settle in for a long, intense series

BY JOHN NIYO

Burning questions Tuesday night following the Wings' 3-2 loss to the Carolina Hurricanes in Game 1 of the Stanley Cup Finals:

Q. The Wings scored the first goal, and still lost?

A. The Wings have scored first 11 times in the playoffs, and that's only the second time they've gone on to lose the game. But, really, though the Wings drew first blood, it was a self-inflicted wound for Carolina.

The Wings' first goal came on a power play, with Sergei Fedorov pocketing the rebound off a Steve Yzerman shot. But add a couple of assists to Tomas Holmstrom, who parked himself in front of goalie Arturs Irbe, and former Wing Aaron Ward, who upended the Demolition Man directly on top of Irbe.

Carolina's goalie had no chance to make a play on Fedorov's shot.

Q. A bad play by Ward?

A. In theory, no. The Hurricanes can't let Holmstrom stand in the crease and screen Irbe, whose biggest weakness at times is the fact that he's only 5-foot-8. But on this one, even Ward admitted he'd have done things differently given a second chance.

"I think if I would've left (Holmstrom), we could have got a penalty there," said Ward, who was booed by the Joe Louis Arena Crowd during pregame introductions.

Q. Not exactly the homecoming he had hoped for, huh?

A. No, but not exactly unexpected, either. In the playoffs, there's no room for friends among foes.

Make no mistake, Ward isn't hated here. The Wings' training staff even sent him a present earlier this season. (Granted, it was a box of doughnuts, poking fun at Ward's struggles to keep his weight down during his Detroit days.)

Ward just didn't fit in Detroit. His relationship with coaches Scotty Bowman and Barry Smith wasn't going to change. Ward is biting his tongue this week, refusing to talk about his frustrating years with the Wings.

But in an Internet column Stan Fischler wrote for Fox Sports, Ward was quoted as saying recently, "(Dave) Lewis is the real coach of the Wings. Scotty is like a figurehead."

Ouch.

Q. Back to the game, how did the Wings lose it?

A. Well, a broken stick might have been the big break the Hurricanes needed.

PHOTO: ALAN LESSIG

Aaron Ward hugs his Carolina teammates after Ron Francis' overtime goal.

In the final minute of the second period, Sergei Fedorov broke his stick behind the Detroit net. Moments later, he smartly cleared the puck with his glove, but then Fedorov hesitated rather than heading to the bench. While Fedorov floated, Ward — there's that name again — made an excellent pass to Jeff O'Neill, streaking behind Fedorov at the blue line. O'Neill ended up with a breakaway goal at 19:10 on a shot that trickled past Hasek.

Q. But that only tied the score, didn't it?

A. Sure did, and a 2-2 tie after two periods is exactly what Carolina was hoping for Tuesday night. At this time of year, the goal on the road is simply to hang around long enough to steal a game. That's particularly true for the Hurricanes, who were 6-1 in overtime in the playoffs and 6-0 in games in which the score was tied after two periods.

Make that 7-0 on the last count. Get ready for a long series, Wings fans.

DRAPER DOES IT!

Kris Draper jumps into the
arms of Darren McCarty after
he gave the Wings a 3-1 lead.

PHOTO: DAVID GURALNICK

Draper, Lidstrom score 13 seconds apart in victory

By Bob Wojnowski

The Red Wings were putting the puck everywhere. High. Wide. Occasionally on net. The chances were coming, then disappearing, and tension was mounting.

Finally, the answer came, in the simplest form: Better aim.

Red Wings	3
Hurricanes	1
Series tied, 1-1	

Nicklas Lidstrom delivered a blast late in the third period that finally found the back of the net behind Carolina goalie Arturs Irbe. It broke a tie and gave the Wings a 3-1 victory in Game 2 of the Stanley Cup Finals, knotting the series at a game apiece. And that breeze you felt about 10:45 Thursday night? That was Hockeytown, sighing in relief.

The Hurricanes were hanging tough, and the signs were growing ominous for the Wings. They were missing chances, wide-open nets, power-play blasts. If Irbe was doing all the puck-dodging, the Wings were doing all the danger-dodging.

"We talked between periods about how we had to keep our composure and not get frustrated," Lidstrom said. "We had to keep at it, and we'd find an opening. It finally paid off for us."

Fittingly, Lidstrom, with one of the team's sharpest shots, found the opening. Sometimes, all it takes is one to get things rolling. Thirteen seconds after Lidstrom's goal, Kris Draper scored on a similar slapper — high to Irbe's glove side — to clinch it. The Wings rebounded nicely from their Game 1 loss, controlling much of the play, but one tone has been set, and I'm not sure it's breakable. This series will defy the advance billing and stay tight.

"Honestly, it wasn't really frustrating because we were playing well," said Wings captain Steve Yzerman.

After two games, we know a little more about these Hurricanes, and the Wings' task. We know they won't go anywhere without a push. We know they'd rather deliver a good shove than a good show. We know one tight game is a sign. Two constitute an official trend.

"We've got to realize this is the kind of series it's going to be," Draper said. "They hang around. They're not going anywhere. We've been in every situation possible as a team, so there's something for us to draw upon."

True enough. Among their myriad lessons, the Wings need to recall this one: Shoot the puck. Um, on the net.

Carolina doesn't give up much. When it does, you can't afford to miss. Late in the first period, with a chance to pad a 1-0 lead, the Wings shot all around Irbe. They shot wide, they shot high (not hard to do with the 5-8 goalie).

There was Chris Chelios, swooping in, big blast, wide. Brett Hull, swooping in, big blast, wide. Yzerman, alone in front, quick blast, wide. The Wings don't mind target practice — but why won't the target stop moving? Carolina's defense is active and physical, adept at blocking shots, tipping shots or ducking shots. Through two periods, the Hurricanes had blocked an astounding 21 shots to the Wings' four.

Defense is the great equalizer in almost any sport, especially in hockey. Sure enough, the underdog Hurricanes are equalizing. This series is getting pretty simple, pretty quickly. Carolina is forcing very little. And the Wings are on middle ice, deciding whether to attack (and possibly commit a mistake) or sit back and play Carolina's style.

Maybe the best thing for the Wings is to tempt the Hurricanes into naughtiness, lure them into offensive aggressiveness. Here's an idea — commit a penalty and put Carolina on the power play!

It's the Wings' version of rope-a-dope. OK, it's not a real strategy, but it worked. With Carolina on a power play, forward Sami Kapanen forced the puck deep, Draper chipped it out, and away the Wings went. On a two-on-one, Kirk Maltby used Lidstrom as a decoy and beat Irbe for the 1-0 lead.

That's how you play a patient style. Yep. And just a few minutes later, Carolina confirmed it with its own short-handed goal.

Fredrik Olausson made a poor play, turning the puck over to former Michigan State standout Rod Brind'Amour, who skated in on the breakaway and scored on a prone Dominik Hasek. That made it 1-1, and just like in the Colorado series, a two-goal lead was looking like a fantasy.

This wasn't end-to-end, brisk-skating hockey. This was try-to-be-aggressive-but-be-careful hockey. This was — dare we say it? — Carolina hockey. It isn't exciting. But it's up to the Wings to adjust because Carolina isn't changing.

It's the perfect answer, maybe the only answer, and it was delivered finally, deep into the third period. Finally, the Wings' aggressiveness was rewarded. Now, they head to Raleigh knowing for sure what this series is all about.

Steve Yzerman celebrates a goal in Game 2.

This shot by Kirk Maltby in the first period found its way into the net for the Wings' first goal.

Hurricanes prove they belong in Stanley Cup Finals

By Rob Parker

In the end, you'll thank the Carolina Hurricanes. And by the time the Stanley Cup Finals are over, the reason will be crystal clear.

In a perfect world, of course, your team, the Red Wings, would stomp the opponent, in this case, the Hurricanes, and it wouldn't even be a series. Most fans, not just die-hard Red Wings fans, wouldn't want to sweat out a game or the outcome of the series, for that matter. A four-game sweep would do just fine. Heck, the Hurricanes, if those fans had their way, wouldn't even score a goal.

But the Hurricanes have legitimized this series by beating the Red Wings in Game 1 and playing tough in a 3-1 Wings victory Thursday night in Game 2 at Joe Louis Arena.

In so doing, they also have given the masses, outside Michigan and North Carolina, a reason to watch and care about this best-of-seven series.

roster with nine potential Hall of Famers on it. They are supposed to win, and win quite easily.

On the other hand, the Hurricanes, despite all their success in the playoffs this season, are viewed as the little train that couldn't. They have some good players, none on a par with the Wings' stars. People didn't expect the Hurricanes to win this series. You'd be hard-pressed to find those people who thought the opposite.

That's not to say the Hurricanes will win the championship just because they won Game 1. It's just that the Wings will have to earn this Cup.

After confidence gained from Game 1, the Hurricanes showed they were ready for Game 2.

"This is a typical game for them," Wings Coach Scotty Bowman said. "It's always tight, it's always close."

Basically, they had already accomplished what most teams would have wanted to do in this kind of series: get a split in Motown. For more than two periods Thursday, they had the Wings on their heels. The last thing the Wings wanted was to be down 0-2 heading to Raleigh, N.C., for the next two games.

It's not that the Wings couldn't come back from such a deficit. It's just that they wouldn't want to make it harder than it really has to be.

It's hard to imagine that any team can beat the Wings in a best-of-seven series. Still, a tougher series will make this wonderful run even more impressive when it's over.

When this team was put together last summer by General Manager Ken Holland, the thought was that it was built to win a Stanley Cup. Anything else would be considered a failure.

Few thought there wouldn't be any bumps in the road en route to June and a big parade downtown.

When the Wings lost the first two games at home against the Canucks in the first round, that was a big bump. They went on to win the next four games for a memorable finish.

But the series that has made this story good reading was the Wings' ability to slay the defending Stanley Cup champion Colorado Avalanche in seven games. Even though Game 7 was disappointing as far as drama goes — a 7-0 Wings victory — it didn't take away what the Wings were able to accomplish. The same seems likely in this case.

In a lot of ways, this series looks like the 1994 Stanley Cup Finals when the New York Rangers beat the Vancouver Canucks in the seventh and deciding game.

Coming into the series, though, it appeared to be a mismatch. The Canucks seemed destined for an early-round playoff exit, not a team with a shot at the Cup. The Rangers, on the other hand, were being led by Mark Messier, a proven winner.

It turned out to be a series to remember. That probably will happen to this series. Thanks to the Hurricanes, that is.

"Both teams are playing for a Stanley Cup, so it's not like anybody is going to give up after a loss, or after a tough period or whatever," Wings captain Steve Yzerman said after the game. "Carolina has generally throughout the playoffs been in low-scoring games with low shots. And that's pretty much what it was in the first two games.

"And we expect it to continue this way."

Even though a Stanley Cup victory is a Stanley Cup victory no matter how you look at it, these Stanley Cup Finals would have been a little tarnished if the Wings had blown out Carolina in Game 1 and appeared en route to a lopsided sweep.

Most would have thought nothing of the events that will take place in the next week or so. After all, the Wings have the highest payroll in the NHL at around $63 million and a

PHOTO: DAVID GURALNICK

Boyd Devereaux hammers Hurricanes defenseman Glen Wesley in the first period.

Underdogs from Carolina bring strong effort again

BY JOHN NIYO

Burning questions Thursday after the Wings' 3-1 victory over the Carolina Hurricanes in Game 2 of the Stanley Cup Finals:

Q: Headed to Carolina with the series tied one game apiece, what have we learned?

A: Essentially this: Carolina isn't going to get out of the Wings' way. Literally, or figuratively.

Early on, Thursday night's contest was eerily reminiscent of Game 5 of the Western Conference finals against Colorado, as the Wings fired shot after shot into opponents' shin pads and stick blades.

After two periods, the NHL officials had the Wings with four blocked shots. The Hurricanes were credited with 21.

Q: What's the problem?

A: The power play is the problem, first and foremost.

The Wings have a couple different strategies they like to use on the power play, but it was painfully clear for most of Thursday's game that the umbrella formation isn't exactly raining shots on Arturs Irbe.

Irbe was slow to react to Nicklas Lidstrom's power-play goal in the third period, thanks in part to Tomas Holmstrom's screen in front.

Still, the Wings desperately need to manufacture more chances with the puck down low, especially the way Irbe is playing. He's been stopping nearly everything he sees for a few weeks now.

Q: Well, it was good to see the stars come out to play, wasn't it?

A: Sure was. Actors John Cusack and Neve Campbell, reportedly a Hollywood couple for a few years now, were in attendance Thursday night.

Q: Huh?

A: Cusack, a Chicago native, is a longtime pal of Chris Chelios and despite some misgivings has softened his Blackhawks allegiance enough to root for the Wings.

Q: Fine but, seriously, how did the Wings' big three perform in this one?

A: They were better, but not necessarily good enough in another penalty-filled game.

Even-strength time is at a premium so far in this series, and Steve Yzerman and Brendan Shanahan have scored one goal apiece in the last nine games. Yzerman's goal was the bank shot off Patrick Roy in Game 5 against Colorado.

Q: How about Carolina's best players?

A: The Wings have done a good job evening things up, stifling the top two lines centered by Ron Francis and Rod Brind'Amour in Game 2. (Brind'Amour's goal Thursday was shorthanded.)

But the play of Carolina's third line, with Josef Vasicek centering Jaroslav Svoboda and Martin Gelinas, remains a concern. That young trio has been effective, overpowering even, when matched against the Wings' third defensive pairing of Mathieu Dandenault and Steve Duchesne.

Yet, it should be noted, Dandenault did draw the penalty against Gelinas that led to Lidstrom's winning goal.

Q: Speaking of penalties, what's the deal with all the whistles?

A: It's hardly a surprise, what with the NHL's game on its biggest stage and trying to produce hockey that reminds viewers of the more wide-open style they saw from the Olympics.

Problem is, the players aren't about to abandon the kind of hockey they've been playing for the last six weeks. So we can expect more of the same as the series shifts to Carolina.

Wings Notebook

BIG MISTAKE: Defenseman Fredrik Olausson was in the lineup for Thursday's Game 2. But he made a type of play that could land him quickly out of the lineup.

Olausson made a grievous first-period error that led to a shorthanded goal for Carolina.

Olausson attempted a cross-ice pass that landed right on the stick of Hurricanes forward Rod Brind'Amour. Alone on a breakaway, Brind'Amour put a puck high into the net past goalie Dominik Hasek to tie the score at 1. Olausson missed Wednesday's practice because of an undisclosed injury, believed to involve his ribs.

SHORTHANDED SKILLS: The Wings proved to be more dangerous shorthanded than they were on the power play during Game 2 of the Stanley Cup Finals Thursday night.

Kirk Maltby scored his second goal of the Finals when he took a pass from Kris Draper in his own end, stickhandled down ice and beat Arturs Irbe with a wrist shot from the right circle in a shorthanded situation at 6:33 of the first period. Maltby's goal was the seventh shorthanded goal of the playoffs for the Red Wings.

HALFWAY HOME!

The Red Wings'
Igor Larionov,
center, celebrates
his winning goal
with teammate
Mathieu
Dandenault.

DANIEL MEARS / THE DETROIT NEWS

Larionov, at age 41, scores winner in third OT, and Hasek is magnificent for Wings in marathon

BY BOB WOJNOWSKI

T he Red Wings were due. Due for a huge goal, due for some overtime magic, due for a break.

The Wings waited, waited, then finally cashed in during the desperate early hours of Sunday morning. Igor Larionov's goal in the third overtime, just past 1 a.m., silenced the Carolina crowd and gave the Wings a 3-2 victory in Game 3 of the Stanley Cup Finals.

The goal, Larionov's second of the game, was a superb individual effort. The triumph nudged the Wings into a 2-1 series lead, and it was a picture of perseverance rewarded. Numerous times, Wings shots ricocheted off posts. Even after Brett Hull tied the game with 1:14 left in regulation, the Wings were persistently dangerous. Keep knocking, keep shooting, something eventually opens.

Red Wings	3
Hurricanes	2
(OT) Wings lead, 2-1	

The Wings again collected the most chances, and missed the most chances. At stake: a 2-1 lead in the Finals. Also at stake: perhaps the Wings' sanity.

The goalies were superb, with Carolina's Arturs Irbe and Detroit's Dominik Hasek alternating superlatives. Agony was etched everywhere. There was Steve Yzerman doing a somersault after Irbe stuffed him in the second overtime.

This was great theater, for the stout-hearted. In the first overtime, the Wings' Pavel Datsyuk just missed the winning goal after making a beautiful move around the defense. Moments later, Brendan Shanahan's shot just wide after taking a perfect pass from Sergei Fedorov. Moments after that, Fredrik Olausson ripped a shot off the crossbar behind Irbe.

The Hurricanes handled almost everything the Wings threw at them, which means the Wings had to find something else to throw. Late in the game, they decided to use a different part of the stick. Hull's delicate redirect of Nicklas Lidstrom's shot tied the score, and merely ratcheted up the tension. Lidstrom followed moments later with a slapper off the post.

But the Wings didn't buckle. They also finally reversed an amazing trend. The victory raised their overtime record in these playoffs to 2-4, and dropped Carolina to 7-2.

The third period of this one was a microcosm of the series. With the score tied 1-1, the Wings were gathering momentum. Steve Duchesne plunked a shot off the post. Yzerman just missed on another chance.

And seconds later, here came Jeff O'Neill, taking a perfect pass from Ron Francis, skating in and beating Hasek for the goal that gave Carolina a 2-1 lead.

For three games now, the Wings occasionally have looked like a team skating through mud. If it's not the mushy ice, it's the mucky Carolina defense. No one denies the Hurricanes are absolutely doing the right thing, the only thing they can to slow the Wings.

It's wonderfully tense. It's tight. It requires accountability and responsibility, but it is painfully dull, no matter how you dress it up.

THE GOALIES WERE SUPERB, WITH CAROLINA'S ARTURS IRBE AND DETROIT'S DOMINIK HASEK ALTERNATING SUPERLATIVES. AGONY WAS ETCHED EVERYWHERE.

The Hurricanes' mascot is a pig on skates. The Wings' primary goal to is to stay out of Carolina's slop, and stay out of the penalty box. That's easier stated than executed. The best way to pull it off is to use this weapon — speed.

It's what makes Sergei Fedorov so valuable. It makes Boyd Devereaux and Kirk Maltby so noticeable this time of year.

Speed makes one of the Wings' underrated players one of their most important. Kris Draper scored the clinching goal in Game 2, and was all over the ice in Game 3. He stole the puck and fed Yzerman, who clanked a shot off the post. Later, Draper had another near-breakaway, and a near-goal.

If you're waiting for your glitzy Wings to break out with a sudden Red Flurry, you might be waiting the entire series. If you're waiting for the Hurricanes to ditch the hog routine and start flying (when pigs fly!), you'll be disappointed.

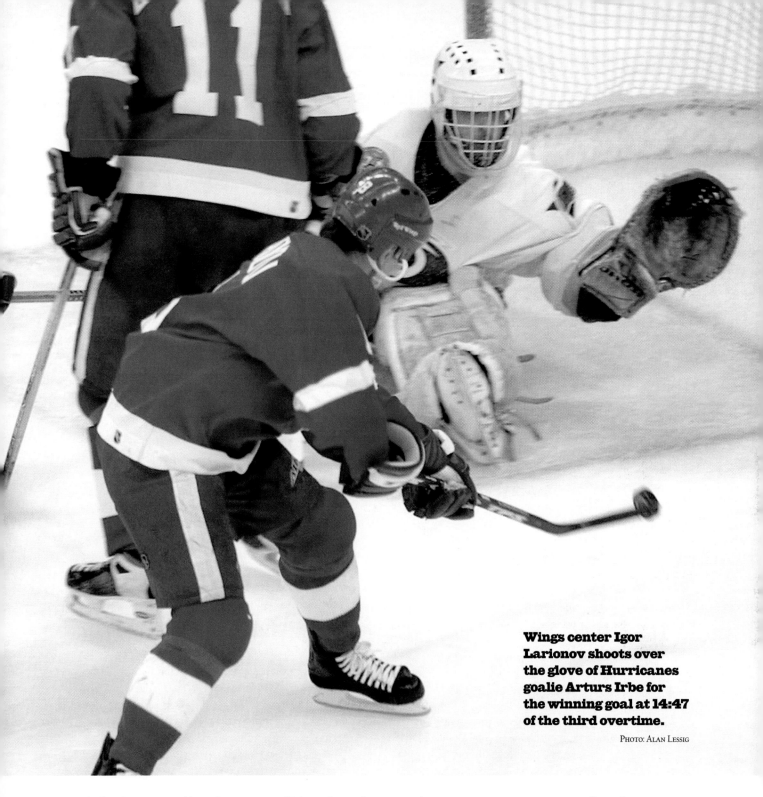

Wings center Igor Larionov shoots over the glove of Hurricanes goalie Arturs Irbe for the winning goal at 14:47 of the third overtime.

PHOTO: ALAN LESSIG

Again, little is being created by either team. It's all about the next mistake, and who makes it. The Wings committed the first big one, when Carolina's Josef Vasicek skated around Steve Duchesne and beat Hasek, who normally makes that save.

The Wings tied it in the second period when Hull swiped the puck from Sean Hill along the boards and sent it out front, where Igor Larionov tapped it past Irbe. Two simple plays. No sustained pressure.

Larionov, at 41, became the oldest player ever to score in a Finals. Fitting. Everyone is aging rapidly in this one.

The Hurricanes like their hockey ugly, even sloppy. The Wings claim they're not frustrated, and maybe they aren't. They continue to get more scoring chances, but Carolina is doing an excellent job forcing the Wings to alter their style, to work extra hard and extra long.

When everyone rubs the sleep from their eyes today, they'll see a series amazingly tight, and a Wings team increasingly sore from all the shooting.

The Red Wings and Hurricanes mix it up behind Detroit's goal during Game 3.

The referees are getting in the way of the games

By John Niyo

Three's company, four is a crowd.

One could argue that has become the underlying theme of the Stanley Cup Finals, a subtle sidelight amid all the penalties.

In Game 2, it was Luc Robitaille colliding with referee Don Koharski, nullifying a would-be wraparound attempt near the Carolina net.

Saturday night's strangest sight was Hurricanes defenseman Sean Hill taking an angry swipe at referee Bill McCreary — their skates were locked in a tangled mess along the boards — while Brett Hull grabbed the loose puck and set up Igor Larionov's second-period goal.

For all the talk about Carolina clogging up the neutral zone, there is this, too: The referees are getting in the way of the Finals.

At issue is the league's two-referee system, where one ref-

eree stays down low and watches the puck while the other ref watches the rest of the play from the neutral zone. It's in its second full season of use after a two-year phase-in period.

But in addition to the aforementioned mishaps with the referees' positioning, there are other criticisms. Among them is the notion that a penalty in one referee's eye at one end of the ice isn't always whistled by the other ref at the other end, leading to confusion among players.

And that might be compounded in these Finals by an apparent crackdown on all the clutching, grabbing, hooking, holding, slashing and various other infractions the league views as detrimental to its growth in popularity with a U.S. television audience.

The first two games in the Finals featured a total of 33 penalties and 29 power plays. There were five more power plays in first period and 15 penalties in regulation Saturday.

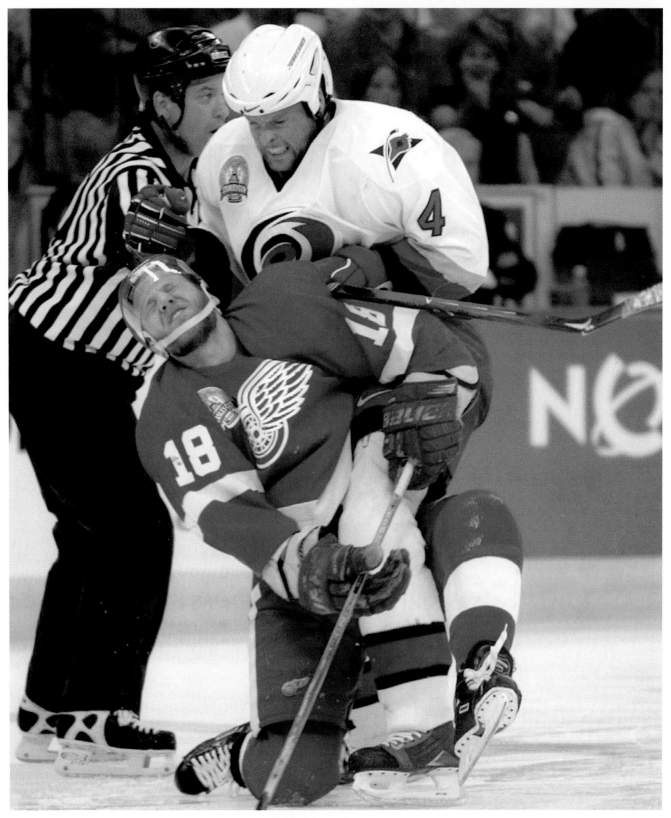

Aaron Ward of the Hurricanes runs into Kirk Maltby. Ward is a former Red Wing.

PHOTO: ALAN LESSIG

Brett Hull, foreground, celebrates after his deflection eluded Arturs Irbe for the tying goal.

Hockeytown fans show their true colors in Carolina

BY ANGELIQUE S. CHENGELIS

Sandy Dornton and Deb Huntley arrived here from Detroit early Saturday morning, and they immediately went to work.

Armed with red markers and an endless supply of paper, the two women created one Red Wings logo after another. Dornton, of Livonia and Huntley, of Pinckney both season-ticket holders, then taped their creations over the Carolina Hurricanes logo that appears on posters that read: One Team, One Dream.

They said this was all part of the good-natured ribbing between Red Wings and Hurricanes fans.

"It's fun, just plain fun," Dornton, who sports a Red Wings tattoo on her left calf, said of following the Wings on the road.

They are part of the group of 160 that traveled here with Mickey Redmond Tours. The travel packages, which include tickets for Games 3 and 4, hotel accommodations and transportation, cost between $1,575 and $2,117 per person.

Hours before the game, the mood was festive at the Comfort Suites where most of the Wings fans are staying.

"Once you've (traveled with the Wings), you get a fever for it," Dave Nowak of Howell said. "You get hooked. You hear about it, you see it on the TV, but actually being there and experiencing it, that's the whole key."

Wings crash party at Carolina's Cup debut

By John Niyo

Burning questions Saturday following Game 3 of the Stanley Cup Finals between the Red Wings and Carolina Hurricanes:

Q. So this is what a Hurricane feels like, huh?

A. The eye of the storm is supposed to be calm and quiet, but the Entertainment & Sports Arena was neither Saturday night.

The noise began even before Carolina skated out — to the Scorpions' "Rock Me Like a Hurricane," of course — and it only got louder when Josef Vasicek danced around Steve Duchesne to beat Dominik Hasek at 14:49 of the first period.

Q. Fine, but is it any different than a game in Detroit?

A. Different, definitely. Blue skies, barbeque grills, thousands of tailgating fans and a rock band outside the arena, for starters. And not an octopus in sight, though there were plenty of Wings jerseys enjoying the party in the parking lot.

Q. Sounds more like a football game, doesn't it?

A. Well, North Carolina State's stadium is only a slapshot away, but these Carolina crazies are a crowd that enjoys hockey, to be sure. They're just having some good ol' American fun with Canada's game.

Q. Strange, then, that the Canadian broadcasters, CBC-TV, bother to show the U.S. national anthem before the game while ABC and ESPN don't, isn't it?

A. It is, yes. A little disappointing, too. But maybe it is ABC's way of making up for all the lost commercial time during the World Cup soccer games.

Q. OK, but what about the hockey games? Are the Wings in trouble in this series?

A. Perhaps, especially if they thought they wouldn't find themselves in this position, though that's not likely.

The Wings, as predicted, are in for a fight, and they knew they would have to win on the road — as they've done all playoffs — to bring home the Cup.

Q. No serious concerns?

A. Oh, there's at least a few. And one became even more apparent Saturday night when Scotty Bowman shuffled his lineup to start the third period with both the game and the series tied.

A big concern is the silence of 30-goal wings Brendan Shanahan and Luc Robitaille, neither of whom has been enough of a scoring threat thus far in the series.

Bowman gave Robitaille a shift alongside Steve Yzerman and Sergei Fedorov early in the third period, hoping to spark Robitaille. He finally got a shot on goal, his first shot to find the net in three games. Bowman then went to Brett Hull with Yzerman and Fedorov with the Wings trailing, a line that might merit another look in Game 4.

Finally, he moved Fedorov back with Lidstrom on the point for an offensive zone faceoff with Hull, Yzerman and Shanahan up front. And that quintet got the tying goal with barely more than a minute left.

Q. So what was the secret?

A. No secret here, but it was Yzerman's faceoff prowess that led to Hull's redirected goal. Yzerman won a faceoff from Rod Brind'Amour, arguably the league's best in the circle. Shanahan and Fedorov helped get the puck back to Lidstrom, and Hull got position on Sean Hill to put his stick on Lidstrom's shot from the blue line.

For Yzerman, it was his fifth faceoff victory in five head-to-head matchups against Brind'Amour. Those are the kind of little victories that eventually lead to big ones.

Wings Notebook

SILENCE IS GOLDEN: Coach Scotty Bowman has decided whether he will return next season to the Red Wings.

He just isn't ready to say what his decision is.

When asked Saturday whether he would have to discuss his future with his family, as he has the last few seasons, Bowman said that wouldn't be necessary.

"No, I have made a decision (about whether to return)," Bowman said. But when asked about the decision, Bowman wouldn't answer.

Bowman, 68, is in his 30th season of coaching. He is showing no signs of slowing down.

General Manager Ken Holland continues to say he has not discussed the matter with Bowman and won't discuss it until after the playoffs are completed.

GOOD PRESSURE: The Wings were pleased with the type of pressure they were able to put on the Hurricanes early in Game 3.

"We had some good sustained pressure," defenseman Mathieu Dandenault said. "They (the Hurricanes) seemed to be running around a little bit. They got some penalties, stuff like that."

VETERANS' DAY

*Experience of Hasek,
Hull and Larionov
too much for Carolina*

Red Wings goalie Dominik Hasek gets tested by Hurricanes captain Ron Francis in the second period, but Francis' shot hit the goalpost and bounced away.

PHOTO: DANIEL MEARS

Hasek is brilliant in net with sixth shutout of playoffs; Wings send message: Hurricane season is ending soon

By Bob Wojnowski

The Red Wings are close, so close now, all they need is the big finish. One more game, maybe one more big goal. Maybe one more wisp of nostalgic magic by one of their venerable stars.

It's all starting to look familiar, isn't it? For the second straight game, the Wings leaned on Brett Hull, the big-game clutch guy, and Igor Larionov, the big-game clever guy. Hull and Larionov scored the huge goals to help the Wings escape Carolina's clutching defense and move within one step of the Stanley Cup.

Red Wings	3
Hurricanes	0
Wings lead, 3-1	

The Wings' 3-0 victory Monday night gave them a 3-1 lead in the Stanley Cup Finals, and showed again, that if one team is to wear down, it won't be the Wings. The Hurricanes might not be done officially, but they look done, mentally, physically and finally.

Game 5 Thursday night at Joe Louis Arena could (should) be the clincher. If it is, no sense in the Wings altering their latest routine. Hull scores first. Larionov follows. Sergei Fedorov, a workhorse marvel, controls much of the game with his skating and passing. Dominik Hasek and Detroit's underrated defense do the rest.

Everyone's on board now, and the Hurricanes have to sense the impending doom. Late in the game, Fedorov's pass to Brendan Shanahan produced the final goal, and it looked suspiciously like a dagger.

"We can't lose our edge now," Steve Yzerman said. "We've been in this situation before, and we've got to come out and play with the same desperation. You just can't get caught up in thinking the series is over."

This Stanley Cup story is being written now by experienced scribblers. Hull, 37, is the self-proclaimed Goat on a line with youngsters Boyd Devereaux and Pavel Datsyuk. Larionov, 41, is the Professor, the oldest player in the NHL.

All that's left is the finishing touch. And really, you can't envision the Wings faltering now, can you?

For the average fan to sit through all the overtimes, to endure tight-checking hockey, to handle the relentless tension, well, that's agony.

For the Wings, there is only fun. Have you noticed it? Have you seen Scotty Bowman's cheerful demeanor? He seems to be enjoying himself more than at any time during the season.

Have you seen the smiles? Hasek, the stoic 37-year-old goalie, laughs easily. This is the sweet price, and no one is happier to pay it these days than Hull.

Hull came here to be one of the Wings' big-goal guys. That's what he was during the regular season, bagging 30 goals. Now, he has become the big-game, big-goal guy. He scored the tying goal with 1:14 left in regulation of Game 3 on a deft stick deflection. And he pulled the Wings from the typical Carolina muck in the second period of this one.

This was the Hull the Wings suspected they were getting when Dallas let him go last summer. Dynamic, effervescent, clutch. In these playoffs, Hull has added a role — The Finisher.

The Finisher does his best work when an opponent is teetering, ready to be pushed. Hull has pushed plenty, leading the Wings with 10 goals in the playoffs. His 10th Monday night — and his 23rd game-winner in the playoffs, ranking second all-time — began the finishing process.

It came at 6:32 of the second period, and it was classic Hull. Devereaux made the nice pass on a two-on-one to Hull, who adopted his standard pose, right knee on the ice, stick poised. His shot slipped past Arturs Irbe and hit the post. Velocity produced the momentum that kept it sliding, into the net.

For Hull, it was his 100th career playoff goal, one of only four NHL players to achieve that. For the Wings, it was one more large step toward escaping the clinging Canes.

"I feel so fortunate, more than you could ever imagine," Hull said. "To be with this group of guys is special, considering back in August, I had nowhere to play."

When the thinnest margin is all that separates these teams, one shot changes everything. Just moments after Hull's goal, Carolina's Ron Francis had almost the exact same chance. He beat Hasek but the puck slid beneath the goalie and clanked off the far post.

Photo: David Guralnick

Sergei Fedorov and Brendan Shanahan celebrate Shanahan's third-period goal as the Wings dominate the Hurricanes, 3-0, in Game 4 in the Stanley Cup Finals.

Maybe then, it began to dawn on the Hurricanes. It's dawning on everyone now. Carolina makes a skilled team like the Wings work for everything, but here's the deal: The Wings are more than willing to do the work, no matter their age, no matter their superstar standing.

You see it in the patient, poised effort. You see it in the smile of Larionov, having the time of his hockey life. His goal, on a perfect pass from Jiri Fischer, provided the elusive two-

goal lead early in the third period. OK, so it wasn't quite as large as Larionov's triple-overtime winner early Sunday.

The energy is growing, so is the lead, so is the feeling. You know the feeling, don't you? The Wings know the feeling, buried for four years as they figured out how to recapture the Cup. They're finding their way back, helped by the Professor and the Goat and everyone else.

Brendan Shanahan beats the Hurricanes' Arturs Irbe in the third period.

Holland's off-season moves look brilliant

By John Niyo

Burning questions Monday night after the Red Wings' 3-0 victory over the Carolina Hurricanes in Game 4 of the Stanley Cup Finals:

Q. Looks like Ken Holland's free-agent moves last summer paid off, eh?

A. They're paying off, yes, and in more ways than one.

Brett Hull certainly has bigger things on his mind, but there is a hidden payday awaiting him if the Wings can finish off the Hurricanes this week.

With his goal in Game 4, Hull joined an elite group — Wayne Gretzky, Mark Messier and Jari Kurri from the Edmonton Oilers' dynasty — as the only players in NHL history with 100 career playoff goals.

But he also got his 10th goal of the playoffs, giving him the outright lead among all NHL players in this postseason. That should be good enough for Hull, who took a sizable pay cut this season, to earn an extra $75,000. There's a bonus clause in his contract that kicks in if he's the league's leading goal-scorer in the playoffs. He gets another $75,000 if the Wings win the Cup.

Colorado's Peter Forsberg and Joe Sakic are second with nine goals apiece. But as any Wings fan will happily note, neither is still in the playoffs. The next closest player threatening Hull's bonus check is Tomas Holmstrom, with seven goals. Carolina's Ron Francis and Erik Cole, and Detroit's Steve Yzerman and Brendan Shanahan, have six goals apiece.

Q. Does anyone else have a financial stake in this?

A. Aside from Mike Ilitch, the next-biggest beneficiary is Dominik Hasek. He has a bonus clause in his contract that pays him $1 million if the Wings win the Stanley Cup. Yzerman would get $150,000, and Shanahan, Chris Chelios and Nick Lidstrom $100,000 each.

Q. Money players, no?

A. Yep, and think about this for a moment.

The biggest goal in the Finals came late in regulation of Game 3, when the Wings forced overtime on Hull's goal. The play came off a faceoff won by Yzerman while Shanahan tied up a defender. Sergei Fedorov passed the puck to Lidstrom, whose shot Hull redirected past goalie Arturs Irbe.

Including Hasek, the six Detroit players on the ice earned a combined salary of $35.5 million this season. (That

PHOTO: DANIEL MEARS

Boyd Devereaux and Brett Hull celebrate after Hull's goal gave the Wings a 1-0 lead.

number is $40 million if one spreads out the Carolina-created bonuses over the life of Fedorov's contract.)

Q. So what does it mean?

A. Well, Hurricanes owner Peter Karmanos probably has a few thoughts on that. His entire team's payroll this season was $33 million.

Q. But it's a young team with a future, no?

A. Sure, but here's another thought on this tired old issue of age. Five of the Wings' last six goals in this series — all the Wings' goals in Carolina before Shanahan's late score Monday — came off the stick of a 37-year-old (Hull) and a 41-year-old (Larionov).

Q. So, do they all ride off into the sunset after one more game?

A. Don't bank on it. All this talk about Wings flying the coop after this season is premature, at the very least. Athletes don't retire easily, and the lure of another championship run will be strong.

So will those big paychecks, by the way.

Igor Larionov fires the Wings' second goal of Game 4 past a diving Arturs Irbe.

Larionov looks ageless again with clutch Game 4 goal

BY ANGELIQUE S. CHENGELIS

Just two days after his heroics in triple overtime in Game 3, Igor Larionov came through again.

Larionov lifted the Red Wings near the end of triple overtime with his goal for a 3-2 victory in the wee hours of Sunday morning. He gave them a cushion Monday night in Game 4 at the Entertainment and Sports Arena, when he scored with 16:17 left in the third period to make it 2-0. The Wings went on to win, 3-0, and take a three-games-to-one lead in the Stanley Cup Finals.

It was the fifth goal of the playoffs and third in the last two games for Larionov, who at 41 is the oldest player in the NHL.

Jiri Fischer set up the score when he got Carolina goalie Arturs Irbe to think he was taking a shot. Instead, Fischer fired a pass to Larionov, who easily scored glove-side. It was Larionov's only shot on goal Monday night.

"Fischer made an excellent pass," said Larionov, who played 22 shifts in 14 minutes, 28 seconds. "I was glad he saw me at the last second and made an excellent pass."

Nicklas Lidstrom said Fischer fooled him with the pass to Larionov.

"Everybody thought he was going to shoot it, and at the last second, he saw Igor," Lidstrom said.

The play was a mix of the young (Fischer) and old (Larionov), and Kris Draper said it proved just how far Fischer has come this season and just how much Larionov's patience comes into play.

"It was a great heads-up play for Fish to see Igor backdoor," Draper said. "Igor just being patient, just hoping for the puck to come and it did. It was two great plays.

"(Fischer) just kind of stood there with the puck and made a great pass. Igor is the kind of guy who searches out little areas and nobody saw him. He kind of got behind everybody, and Fish made a great play to get it over to him. Patience can't be taught and that's something Igor has."

Red Wings captain Steve Yzerman is tripped up by Carolina's Rod Brind'Amour and Bret Hedican.

Wings Notebook

FISCHER HIT UNDER REVIEW: Red Wings defenseman Jiri Fischer's cross-check of Hurricanes forward Tommy Westlund, which knocked out several of Westlund's teeth but did not draw a penalty, will be reviewed today by the NHL front office.

Fischer hit Westlund near the Wings' net during the third period of the Wings' 3-0 victory Monday night. Westlund was bloodied and needed five stitches to close a cut to his mouth.

"I don't know how many teeth he (Westlund) has got left, but he's fine," Hurricanes Coach Paul Maurice said.

NHL vice-president Colin Campbell will review the play. Replays showed the hit, but the on-ice officials were looking away from the area where it happened.

DEFENSIVE DEMONS: The Wings were successful in shutting down the Hurricanes and taking their boisterous crowd out of the game.

Goalie Dominik Hasek extended his record of playoff shutouts to six, making 17 saves. But he wasn't tested much.

"This was a team shutout more than anything," Hasek said.

CHAMPIONS!

Wings' championship a once-in-a-lifetime experience

By Bob Wojnowski

The noise grew and grew, starting last summer, through the season, through the playoffs, an insistent demand that had to be met. And then it crested on a joyous Thursday night in Joe Louis Arena, ear-splitting and validating.

The final blast was Brendan Shanahan's long shot that found an empty net, and filled a Cup, and lit the crowd. The Red Wings'

Red Wings	3
Hurricanes	1
Wings win, 4-1	

3-1 victory over Carolina ended the Stanley Cup Finals the only way it could end. It ended the season the only way it could, with the Wings' third championship since 1997.

And in a bittersweet twist, it ended the career of Scotty Bowman, who announced afterward he had coached his final game. Bowman, who began contemplating retirement during the Olympic break in February, whispered the news to players as he hugged them on the ice. Then he received the Stanley Cup from captain Steve Yzerman and took a brief, final skate.

"I enjoyed the year, but it's a long, tough grind," Bowman said. "The tough part was leaving the players. But I think it's time. I know it's time."

And now we know, this team of Hall-of-Famers and this season of momentous expectations truly was a once-in-lifetime thing, never to be duplicated.

The last opponent, like the ones before, fell stubbornly. But Carolina fell surely, pushed by a team that was pushed by pressure and its own explicit demands. In the end, it became simple.

The Wings had to have this Cup. They had to have to it. So if no one would hand it to them, they went ahead and took it.

When Yzerman grabbed it and lifted it, another party-splashed Hockeytown summer commenced. Contrary to one of the story lines, this championship was earned, not purchased.

"What's the word for being really happy and really tired?" Yzerman said as he stood on the ice, as pieces of confetti still fluttered. "Exultation? Is that it? That's the way I feel right now. I never really felt uptight during the playoffs because I always felt we were going to win. This is the most-rewarding of the Cups, maybe because I've been through it and could enjoy it."

It was earned by everyone. It was earned by Yzerman, whose right knee ached more than anyone could say publicly. He said after the game he'd undergo reconstructive surgery within a month and be out 4-6 months.

It was earned by Dominik Hasek, a single-minded goalie who represented this team's single purpose. It was earned by Nicklas Lidstrom, the smooth defenseman who won the Conn Smythe Trophy for playoff MVP. And of course, it was earned by Bowman, Legend Personified, who broke the NHL record with his ninth title.

For the final three minutes, the crowd shouted, "We want the Cup!" It was the chant of the night, of the series, of the year.

So many goals, one goal. Nothing less than the Cup. So many goals on the roster, so many personal goals, but this season was about one goal, ever since the Wings signed Hasek, Brett Hull and Luc Robitaille last summer.

They finished off the pesky Hurricanes with all the familiar elements. There was Tomas Holmstrom, the guy who merely takes all the punishment, then delivers the biggest goals, poking in a perfect pass from Igor Larionov for the game's first score.

There was Sergei Fedorov controlling the puck, then feeding Shanahan for one of his classic slappers, and a 2-0 lead.

The Hurricanes would not go quietly, but then, no one has against the Wings. Jeff O'Neill's power-play goal late in the second period sliced the deficit, and set up just a bit more tension.

Why not? The Wings had skated with it all of the playoffs, and much of the season. Nothing less than the Cup. Nothing.

Beyond the obvious talent, something always drives a championship team. In '97, the Wings were pushed by the ache of history, to end the 42-year drought and get the Captain his first Cup. By the end, they were unbeatable, sweeping Philadelphia.

In '98, the Wings were pushed by the ache of mortality. The limousine accident that severely injured defenseman Vladimir Konstantinov and masseur Sergei Mnatsakanov stirred the deepest emotions. By the end, the Wings were unbeatable, sweeping Washington.

This year's team had no singular cry, just a singular goal. You knew it, they knew it, everyone knew it. They had to win, or their high-priced push would be mocked across the hockey world. This was about skating with the heaviest expectations, hurriedly molding Hall of Fame credentials into a team, and fulfilling personal goals.

For Yzerman, this was about completing his greatest challenge. He took painkiller shots before every game. But after the surgery, he said he'll be back.

Nicklas Lidstrom became the first European to win the Conn Smythe Trophy.

For the franchise, this stamps it with the largest validation. A third Cup pushed the Wings past contemporaries Colorado (two) and New Jersey (two). Yzerman talked before the play-offs about the importance of paying back Owner Mike Ilitch for having faith in his veterans to go for it again.

For Ilitch and General Manager Ken Holland, this is the payoff they gambled on when they signed Hasek, Hull and Robitaille. Today, they celebrate. But at the time, Ilitch risked financial disaster, as well as the resentment of fellow owners. Besides pushing economic barriers, he was pushing age barriers, building the league's oldest roster.

For Bowman, this was the most-personal ring, the ninth, the one that lifted him past his idol, Toe Blake. It cemented Bowman, 68, as the greatest coach in the game, maybe the greatest in all sports.

For Hasek, this was the moment he had to have, to truly be considered one of the finest goalies of all time. He needed the Wings to win his first Cup; they needed him. No sense ending the relationship after one year, right, Dominator?

For Fedorov and Lidstrom, who somehow remain both brilliant and underrated, this was the year they finally, truly were appreciated. If Yzerman is the heart, these guys form the backbone.

For Shanahan, the original Missing Piece, this was the season of determined accomplishment. For Chris Chelios, 40, and Igor Larionov, 41, this was profound evidence that age truly means nothing.

For the Grind Line — Kris Draper, Darren McCarty, Kirk Maltby — this was more of what they provide, at their best. Energy, enthusiasm and the occasional monstrous goal.

At the end, the Wings were nearly as dominant as their championship predecessors. There was no Finals sweep against a dogged Carolina team, although they did finish with four straight victories. And there were those high-danger moments — down two games to Vancouver, down three games to two to Colorado.

We know where this began, this latest quest for the Cup. It began on a spring night in Los Angeles, just a year ago, when the Wings lost a fourth straight game in the first round to the Kings, with players injured and the defense collapsing. The evidence was indisputable. The Wings needed help.

The pieces fit. The pieces fit so tightly, you can barely pry them apart. To pick a most valuable player is fruitless, and it's designed that way. This wasn't a team that won with a hot goalie, or a scoring star. It won with superstars playing roles, and role players playing stars.

It won the way it had to win, the only way it could. So many goals, one goal. The Wings grabbed them all, and deserved them all. And now, the noise makes perfect sense.

Scotty Bowman won the Stanley Cup for the ninth time in his career and the third time with the Red Wings.

PHOTO: JOHN T. GREILICK

Don't underestimate Ilitch's role in success

By John Niyo

Burning questions Thursday night following the Red Wings' 3-1 victory over the Carolina Hurricanes in Game 5 of the Stanley Cup Finals:

Q. As Detroit prepares for another championship parade, who should be the grand marshal?

A. That's easy. It should be the man who had the most at stake in these playoffs: Mike Ilitch.

Accolades fluttered like confetti Thursday night in a jubilant, champagne-soaked dressing room at Joe Louis Arena, and all involved certainly deserved a share of the credit.

But on the morning of Game 5, it was Scotty Bowman, in one of his last acts as coach, who properly acknowledged what made it all possible.

Bowman was asked what the common denominator was between legendary coaches such as himself, Red Auerbach and Phil Jackson. The Wings' coach, who tied both NBA men with his ninth title as head coach, didn't have an answer. But in hockey, he said, there are two key players: the franchise goaltender and the franchise owner.

"It hasn't happened often where the owner (of a championship team) isn't probably the biggest fan of the team," Bowman said. "And this owner here, I mean, to do what he did last summer."

Indeed, to shell out $65 million in salaries, it's fair to say Ilitch earned the right to strut down Woodward Avenue if he chooses.

Q. Three championships in six years makes a dynasty, no?

A. Probably not, especially with the payroll disparity in this era of NHL free agency.

Make no mistake, this Detroit team truly is an impressive collection of future Hall of Fame players, even if many of them are in the twilight of their careers.

But it might be a reach to place this team right alongside the Edmonton Oilers and New York Islanders teams of the 1980s, and certainly Bowman's teams in Montreal in the 1970s. Bowman, in fact, will be the first to tell you that.

Still, this was a team that will be remembered for a long time, both for what it was and what it did.

Q. More important, what will the Wings do for an encore?

A. The simple answer? It will keep winning.

Expect the Wings to be Cup contenders again next season, though probably not the favorites — not with Peter Forsberg back for a full season in Colorado.

PHOTO: DAVID GURALNICK

Said 40-year-old Chris Chelios: "This was amazing to hold the Cup up like that. ... This is incredible, I can't even describe it all."

But Wings management, buoyed financially by this year's success, will plug the necessary holes through free agency — Curtis Joseph? Bobby Holik? Bill Guerin? — as well as from within.

In particular, the front office is eager to see Henrik Zetterberg in a Wings uniform, and he'll join a more physically prepared Pavel Datsyuk and Jason Williams to provide youth up the middle. On defense, it's time to see if Maxim Kuznetsov and Jesse Wallin are ready to contribute.

Q. Speaking of contributions, are there any that haven't been properly recognized?

A. A few, as always, but why not start with Tomas Holmstrom, whose ice-breaking goal Monday night was his eighth of the playoffs.

That's a career high — he had seven in the 1998 Stanley Cup run — and it's certainly impressive on its own. But it's even more so when one considers the physical abuse he takes through two months of playoffs. Consider this, too: He managed only eight goals in three times as many games (69) in the regular season.

Talk about a playoff performer.

Bowman's retirement announcement shocks Hockeytown fans

By Angelique S. Chengelis

Moments after winning a record ninth Stanley Cup, Red Wings Coach Scotty Bowman ended speculation and announced his retirement.

"I made up my mind in February at the Olympic break ... (it's) just too much," Bowman, 68, said Thursday night after taking the ice to celebrate the Wings' Stanley Cup championship following a 3-1 victory over the Carolina Hurricanes at Joe Louis Arena. "Other years, I never was sure, but after a couple weeks, I wanted to come back, especially the last three years.

"I know it's time now. I didn't know it was time then. I just felt it was time."

Captain Steve Yzerman, whom Bowman informed of his decision on the ice after the game, accepted the Stanley Cup from Commissioner Gary Bettman and then handed it to Bowman, who hoisted the Cup above his head and skated briefly to the cheers of the packed arena.

"I have many people to thank, but the first person I have to thank, obviously, is my wife (Suella) who stood right beside me for the last 30-plus years," said Bowman, who has five children. "I also have to say a special thank-you to Sam Pollock, because 46 years ago he gave me my first job in hockey in Ottawa."

Bowman, already in the Hockey Hall of Fame, completed nine seasons with the Red Wings and has three Stanley Cups, including titles in 1997 and 1998, with the organization.

He has 10 Cups overall, but his nine as a head coach break the record set by legendary Toe Blake, who coached Montreal to eight Cups.

He said he told only two or three confidants he knew could keep the secret. He did not tell his players until after Thursday's game, while they hugged and congratulated one another.

"I had a lot of confidence in this team," Bowman said. "I made up my mind I was going to work as hard as I can. I didn't want it to be a distraction. I never told any of them, because I didn't feel it was what they wanted to hear anyway. Maybe some of them would have, who knows."

Nicklas Lidstrom, the Conn Smythe Trophy winner, said Bowman told him on the ice that he was retiring.

Photo: Alan Lessig

Scotty Bowman and Steve Yzerman celebrate a Stanley Cup title for the third time.

"He said, 'I've coached my last game,' " Lidstrom said. "I said, 'Let's talk about it. Let's not get ahead of ourselves.' I'd like to see him come back."

Igor Larionov was told by Bowman as the Cup was brought out to the ice.

"I said I was sad," Larionov said. "He is a great coach and we will miss him."

Chris Chelios, perhaps in denial, said he wasn't buying the retirement talk.

"I don't believe a word of it," Chelios said. "People retire and unretire quickly. I'm waiting to see if he means it."

Dominik Hasek races to meet Chris Chelios as time runs out on the Wings' 3-1 victory.

Wings Notebook

ROBITAILLE THRILLED:
Forward Luc Robitaille lingered on the ice longer than almost any player. His wife and two sons were by his side. The joy on their faces was unmistakable.

Robitaille finally had his first Stanley Cup in a Hall of Fame career. He was basking in the joy.

"This is unbelievable," Robitaille said after the Wings won the Cup with a 3-1 victory over the Carolina Hurricanes in Game 5.

"I don't even know what to say," Robitaille said. "I've been waiting for this my entire career. I don't even know what to say. This is incredible." Robitaille, a longtime Los Angeles King, stayed in Detroit while his family remained on the West Coast.

"There was a lot of sacrifice," Robitaille said. "This makes it all worthwhile."

DUCHESNE SPEECHLESS:
Robitaille's good friend, defenseman Steve Duchesne, was another first-time Stanley Cup winner Thursday.

"I've waited 16 long years for this," said Duchesne, who played some of his best hockey of the season during the playoffs.

Ted Kulfan

Stanley's Back!

Scotty Bowman

In 1998, *Sports Illustrated* said Scotty Bowman was the "best coach ever in a major professional sport."

Simply the best

Bowman sets all-time NHL coaching record with ninth Cup, passes his mentor, Toe Blake

By John Niyo

In the midst of this playoff run, one that will stand as perhaps the most gratifying of Scotty Bowman's long, storied career, the 68-year-old Hall of Fame coach was asked whether he leaned on the past in tough times and dire straits.

"I think about it myself," Bowman admitted, pausing as he answered the question. "But how do you know if history is going to repeat?"

Indeed.

Riddle me this, he seemed to be saying. But for all the jokes, for all the eccentricities, for all the maddening tactics, this is Bowman's greatest trick: He keeps repeating himself.

Ten Stanley Cup rings, including nine as head coach. Untouchable NHL records for victories in the regular season (1,244), the playoffs (222) and the Stanley Cup finals (36).

He was dubbed by Sports Illustrated in 1998 the "best coach ever in a major professional sport." And it became harder every year, though this one would be Bowman's last, to quibble with that choice.

A day after Phil Jackson won his ninth NBA championship — tying the coaching record for the four major sports held by Red Auerbach of the Boston Celtics —

Photo: David Guralnick

EVERY SPRING, THE MEDIA FLIRT WITH THE NOTION THAT BOWMAN MIGHT RETIRE, EVEN WHEN HE SHOWS FEW SIGNS OF SLOWING DOWN.

Bowman did the same, nearly 30 years after winning his first title. He laced up his skates — just as he had after winning the Cup in 1997 — and skated out to shake hands and finally tell his players, one by one, that he'd decided to call it quits.

145

PHOTO: DAVID GURALNICK

Scotty Bowman has the record for most victories in the regular season, playoffs and the Finals.

"It's bittersweet," admitted Dave Lewis, a Wings assistant for the last 14 seasons. "He told me after he got his skates on, it was the last game he was going to coach. He said it matter-of-factly, but I think those were the hardest words he's ever spoken."

The words carried some weight, to be sure. Bowman is an icon in a sport that, unlike basketball, clings to its tradition, and that was evident even as the Stanley Cup Finals paid a visit to Tobacco Road this spring.

The Carolina Hurricanes were coached by Paul Maurice, who also happened to be the NHL's youngest coach. And he was, admittedly, living a dream.

"And this is part of that dream that, when you get to the Stanley Cup Finals, the guy on the other bench would be Scott Bowman," said Maurice, a 35-year-old who was born in the same year, Bowman landed his first NHL coaching job.

The year was 1967, and Bowman, a rookie head coach with the expansion St. Louis Blues, reached the Cup Finals for the first time that season. This season, he made his lucky 13th trip.

And, not surprisingly, for Bowman, the Cup Finals are all

"HE WAS FAR AND AWAY THE BEST COACH WHO EVER COACHED IN THE LEAGUE. TOE BLAKE COACHED 13 YEARS IN THE LEAGUE AND WON EIGHT STANLEY CUPS. I'VE HAD 30-SOME YEARS AT IT. IF YOU STAY LONG ENOUGH IN A JOB, YOU GET YOURSELF IN THAT POSITION."

Scotty Bowman, speaking about his coaching mentor, Toe Blake

Photo: David Guralnick

Steve Yzerman, right, on Scotty Bowman: "I've really enjoyed the nine years he has been here."

about memories. Countless memories, in fact, though Bowman, with a mind like a steel trap, seems to have total recall, ticking of experiences the way one might a grocery list.

After the Wings' loss in Game 1 of the Finals against Carolina, it was Bowman providing a little levity — and historical perspective — the following afternoon, while reporters worked feverishly to find out what was wrong with his team and its All-Star lineup.

Bowman harkened back to the 1979 playoffs, when his three-time defending champion Montreal team was in the Finals again against the New York Rangers, an underdog not unlike Carolina this spring.

"The Rangers were a bit of a Cinderella team," Bowman remembered. "I know (Rangers goaltender) John Davidson, he was playing lights-out in the playoffs. But we were pretty excited, pretty confident to have a team that won three Cups in a row."

And pretty well stunned when the upstart Rangers came into the Montreal Forum on a Sunday afternoon and whipped Hall of Fame goalie Ken Dryden and the Canadiens, 4-1.

"We didn't know what the hell happened," Bowman said. "I mean, it was such a crisis we were going to take out Dryden in the next game."

But then came the punch line from Bowman. In warm-ups before Game 2 of that '79 Finals series, Montreal's Doug Risebrough fired a shot that knocked backup goalie Michel Larocque flat on his back, effectively ending any discussion about benching Dryden.

"I always thank Riseborough about it," said Bowman, chuckling at the memory. "Dryden went in and won four straight games."

And Bowman had his fifth Stanley Cup championship, a ring for each of his children. That's what he plans to do with all the Stanley Cup rings when his career is over, give them all to his kids. Heck, he's even got enough for the grandkids -

Scotty Bowman doesn't get close to his players, but he does get impressive results.

another will arrive in August.

When will it end? That's the question that had dogged Bowman since he and the Wings ended a 42-year championship drought, on June 7, 1997.

Every spring, the media flirted with the notion that Bowman might retire, even when the old coach showed little sign of slowing down. Only days before he skated one last time with the Cup, Bowman was asked again about his future, asked if he would need to take some time after the Finals to decide. Bowman raised a few eyebrows with his answer.

"No," Bowman said. "I have made a decision."

But that's as far as he would go, of course: Always keeps 'em guessing.

Certainly, though, he could have kept going if he had wanted. Since his heart angioplasty and knee-replacement surgery after the 1998 season, Bowman has maintained his physical fitness with a prescribed training regimen and improved diet. He hits the treadmill in morning, and he would snack on fruit — no more pizza — after games.

In between, it was a heaping helping of hockey. Bowman committed every imaginable statistic to memory, from travel time and practice schedules to defensive-zone face-off percentages and the number of points the fifth-place team in the West Division had in the 1967-68 season.

In the playoffs, as he tap danced around the media's prying questions, those stats came tumbling out like spilled

To improve his health, Scotty Bowman started snacking on fruit instead of pizza.

beans, but reporters knew reading between the lines with Bowman was like reading tea leaves.

After the 3-2 overtime loss to Carolina in Game 1, Bowman's off-day press conference included a smorgasbord of numbers ranging from the Wings' incomplete passes in the first period, combined power-play time in the game and scoring chances created off the forecheck — in the Carolina-Toronto series, no less.

A few days before that, however, it was Bowman, with a straight face, insisting, "I never worry about records."

That was in response to a question about his mentor, Toe Blake, who coached Montreal to eight Stanley Cups in the 1950s and 60s. And to those who suggested Bowman was hanging around simply to surpass Blake's coaching standard for excellence, the jut-jawed apprentice would shake his head.

The two used to have offices down the hall from each other in the old Montreal Forum. Blake, the game's first — and best — innovator, coached the Montreal Canadiens, while Bowman coached the Montreal Junior Canadiens. They would chat after practices, and Bowman still cherishes his first Stanley Cup Finals appearance with St. Louis in 1968, even though his expansion team lost four straight. That's because the opponent was Montreal, and those four games were the last Blake coached in the NHL. By way of symmetry, Bowman retired after winning four straight, too.

"But he was far-and-away the best coach who ever coached in the league," Bowman said. "Toe Blake coached 13 years in the league and won eight Stanley Cups. I've had 30-some years at it. If you stay long enough in a job, you get yourself in that position."

You stay long enough, too, and you wear out your welcome, more often than not. But Bowman's players in Detroit grew comfortable living with a legend.

Steve Yzerman was asked during the playoffs to share his secret for getting along with Bowman.

Yzerman's reply: "Show up, work hard, and keep your mouth shut. Simple as that."

Granted, it took awhile for the Wings — Yzerman included — to get to that point. Bowman, on the surface, appears to be such a complicated man. And the tension between Bowman and the Wings' captain very nearly resulted in Yzerman getting traded to Ottawa before the 1995-96 season.

But the two managed to live happily ever after.

"I've really enjoyed the nine years he has been here," Yzerman said. "He doesn't get real close to the players. He's not the kind of coach that opens his door and allows you to come in and chat. He's very business-like: You show up when you're expected to, you do what you're expected to do and let the coaches coach.

"With a bunch of older guys on our team we're kind of given a little extra room to do what we want — when we want — off the ice, but there's no question that it's his team."

His team. His legacy. In the end, it was a good marriage for both.

Scotty Bowman
Passed Toe Blake with NHL-record ninth Cup as coach.

Steve Yzerman
Named Red Wings captain in 1986-87, when he was 21.

Photo: Alan Lessig

Nicklas Lidstrom
Defenseman won Norris Trophy in 2001, Conn Smythe of 2002 playoffs.

Brendan Shanahan
Led Wings in scoring with 75 points in 2001-02.

Sergei Fedorov
Three Stanley Cups followed Hart Trophy in 1994.

Chris Chelios
Second Stanley Cup; first was with Montreal in 1986.

Igor Larionov
Oldest player in NHL scored twice in Game 3 of 2002 Finals, once in Game 4.

PHOTO: DANIEL MEARS

Dominik Hasek
Won Vezina Trophy six times before getting Cup.

PHOTO: DAVID GURALNICK

Brett Hull
Scored more than 50 goals five times in NHL career.

PHOTO: ANKUR DHOLAKIA

Luc Robitaille
High-scoring wing notched 600th goal during 2001-02 season.

"WHAT'S THE WORD FOR BEING REALLY HAPPY AND REALLY TIRED?" EXULTATION? IS THAT IT? THAT'S THE WAY I FEEL RIGHT NOW. I NEVER REALLY FELT UPTIGHT DURING THE PLAYOFFS BECAUSE I ALWAYS FELT WE WERE GOING TO WIN. THIS IS THE MOST-REWARDING OF THE CUPS, MAYBE BECAUSE I'VE BEEN THROUGH IT AND COULD ENJOY IT."

Steve Yzerman

PHOTO: DANIEL MEARS